GUIDE

Museo de Bellas Artes

Seville

JUNTA DE ANDALUCIA
CONSEJERIA DE CULTURA

Aldeasa

CONTENTS

It is the duty of every state to provide its citizens with the best means of access to an under-
standing of the world of culture.

We can therefore congratulate ourselves on having in our hands a very special book, the read-
ing of which will lead us through the visual history of Spain.

Furthermore, through this guide to Seville's Museo de Bellas Artes *the commitment made
to all Andalusian citizens in the "General Plan of Cultural Assets" – a document essential
to our Autonomous Community's heritage trusteeship – is fulfilled.*

This museum is the cornerstone of a history that is still very much alive and which began in
the foundations of the old Monastery of La Merced long before the discovery of America. It
is also a storehouse for our cultural treasures, containing examples of the work of Velázquez's
predecessors, teachers and descendants.

Here, any work is important per se, *for its history is also important. Each item, each painting and sculpture, has its own place in the artistic path of the life of Spain. Through the
paintings in the museum we can discover life as it was before our time – its customs, figures,
wars, celebrations, landscapes, feelings, loves and hates. Spanish life over the centuries
through the paintbrushes and chisels of the artists of each age.*

From now on Seville's Museo de Bellas Artes *– Spain's second national gallery – will have
a place in the home of all those who own this book, a unique testimony to the heritage of all
Andalusians. It is a heritage to watch over, not only in the name of those who came before
us or of future generations but also in the representation and trusteeship of all mankind.*

Carmen Calvo Poyato
Counsellor for Culture

MUSEO DE BELLAS ARTES

THE MUSEUM OF SEVILLE

A long history of over 160 years marks the daily development of the life of this picture gallery considered the second greatest in Spain. The Museum's origins lie in the situation which, in the early 19th century, prevailed in a Spain torn between memories of the Enlightenment and Modernity, dreams of past greatness and the Napoleonic invasion, poverty and nobility... Such was the situation, and the records of the birth of the Museum of Seville bear testimony to it.

History of the Museum

The earliest circumstance in the Museum's foundation dates back to 1820, when monasteries with monastic orders, canons regular, etc., were abolished, and a Royal Order of 16th September established a museum in Seville's old Franciscan College of San Bonaventura (a highly inappropriate choice of premises) to house numerous works of art — which would soon be neglected and forgotten. The most recent circumstance dates back to events in Spanish history fifteen years later, when, during the reign of Isabella II, Mendizábal's government ordered the disentailment of the assets of a large number of ecclesiastical institutions. Immediately after this, a Royal Decree of 16th September 1835 established a "Museum of Paintings" in Seville to house requisitioned works of art. At the same time a Commission of prominent Sevillians led by Manuel López Cepero, Dean of the Cathedral, was set up, its task being to assemble a collection of paintings and sculptures worthy of exhibition in the nascent Museum.

The Commission's first assignment was to find suitable premises for the institution. In 1837,

however, the Commission was replaced by another under José María Amor whose members included López Cepero and the painter Antonio Cabral Bejarano (subsequently the gallery's first director). As a site had still not been found, the call for one became ever more urgent. Finally, on 7th October 1839, the gallery was assigned the old Monastery of La Merced Calzada (its current premises), although for years it was obliged to share facilities with other Sevillian cultural and educational institutions. Work on the conversion of the building was begun at once under the supervision of the Provincial Commission for Monuments, while in the meantime Cabral Bejarano drew up the first inventory of the Museum's holdings and the architect Marrón began work on a new boulevard and square to enhance the site. With the passing of time, the

Tiling in the Patio de los Bojes.

square was to become the Plaza del Museo with its statue of Murillo by Sabino Medina.

As Amador de los Ríos recorded, by 1844 the Museum occupied five large rooms in the La Merced building, one being the old church, which was solemnly inaugurated by the Queen as the Murillo Room on 21st September 1862. The existence of the Museum of Seville thus became assured. The holdings were further increased in 1868 in the wake of the Revolution and the 19th-century-style Museum became, according to Gestoso, "The finest provincial museum in the land, all under the supervision of the *Real Academia de Bellas Artes* of Seville, which has, moreover, renovated the cloisters, gardens, galleries, etc." In this manner the Museum crossed the threshold of a new century which was to see the creation of a Board of Trustees (1925), its promotion to the ranks of the great state museums and, above all, a series of efficacious works of consolidation and remodelling culminating in a new installation of the collections presented at a solemn ceremony in the presence of Their Majesties the King and Queen of Spain on 29th May 1993.

In 1984, management of the Museum was transferred to the government of the Autonomous Community of Andalusia, which modernized the Museum in all its aspects, thus raising it to its present status as a great centre of Andalusian culture.

The assembling of the collection

From the very beginning it was understood that the Museum's collection should consist of "provincial" works of art produced by the so-called Sevillian school — a fact which would at first seem to relegate the Museum to a second-class status. Why then do its holdings form one of the "great" collections and why is it Spain's second most-important gallery? The answer is very simple: among the members of the Sevillian school — the main source of the holdings from the city's two great creative periods — were such prominent *Baroque* artists as Francisco Pacheco, Juan de las Roelas, Alonso Cano, Diego Velázquez, Francisco de Zurbarán, Bartolomé Murillo and Juan de Valdés Leal and such *19th-century* artists as Antonio Esquivel, José García Ramos, José Villegas and Gonzalo Bilbao. In this respect it is also important to remember the three great stages in the assembly of the collection — periods reflected in the corresponding inventories published by the gallery's supervisory institutions.

The Museum's initial collection consisted of the original works of 1820 but it was soon swelled by the huge number of items assigned to it in 1840 in the wake of the 1835 Disentailment Act. It was at this time that the first inventory of the Museum's paintings was made. Though never published, the inventory was compiled by the Museum's first director and is now in the Museum's archives. It lists a total of 2,045 works of art of all kinds which with time (as can be seen in the subsequent inventories and catalogues drafted by those in charge of the institution) were screened and considerably reduced in number.

There then followed a second important stage in the Museum's history which might be described as the "consolidation of the collections". Its beginning coincided with the new Disentailment Act of 1868 and came at a time when the number of works of art in the collection was no more than 400, for quantity had given way to quality and the main body of the collection consisted of works by the great Sevillian painters of the 17th century,

(Opposite) The Main Cloister.

particularly Murillo. This is reflected in the first catalogue, published by the Seville *Real Academia de Bellas Artes* in 1850 (with further editions in 1868, 1880 and 1888). The process of selection and consolidation reached a peak in 1912, when the Seville *Academia* published another catalogue of the paintings and sculptures at the Museo Provincial drafted by the academician José Gestoso y Pérez.

The prestige of those in charge of the Museum — with the painter Gonzalo Bilbao as Chairman of the Board of Trustees and the researcher Cayetano Sánchez Pineda as Director — together with the vital support of the authorities, who declared it an "Institution of Public Interest", was to lead to the most recent stage in the assembly of the permanent collection. This was the time of the great donations, the first being that of the works of José Villegas Cordero, bequeathed by the artist's widow in 1921, and the second — important not only due to the large number of works but also to their high quality — that of the Rafael González Abreu legacy of 1928. Shortly after, in 1931, the researcher José Gestoso bequeathed his private collection to the Museum, as did Mr and Mrs Siravegne-Lomelino in 1944 and Andrés Parladé, Count of Aguiar, in 1945. A host of generous Sevillians followed their lead, the result being a noteworthy increase in the number of works of art belonging to the Museum which enabled a complete study of the museography and of the pieces to be made in 1970. It was at this point that the task of "filling the gaps" in the collection began with the acquisition of works by the Spanish state — a task which the Government of Andalusia's Department of Culture has made its own for the last fifteen years. The result has been an extremely impor-

tant one for the Museum: between 1975 and 2000, 31 works of art have been acquired, 12 by the State and 19 by the Autonomous Community Government, so that the Museum currently possesses 1,416 paintings, 340 sculptures and 531 examples of work of the decorative and sumptuous arts. Fortunately, even today a number of private benefactors donate works of art to the Museum of Seville, and in this respect we cannot neglect to mention the Friends of the Museum Association, founded in 1982, whose enthusiasm in acquiring works of art and providing funds for restoration work and cultural events has proved invaluable.

An architectural gem

The Museum is housed in the old Monastery of La Merced Calzada building — the famous *Casa Grande* or "Great House" of the Mercedarians, founded, according to tradition, by St Peter Nolasco immediately after the conquest of the city on land ceded by Ferdinand III the Saint in the orchards of San Laureano, near the River Guadalquivir and the Royal Gate. The monastery was constructed principally of brick in the contemporary 13th-century Mudéjar-Gothic style.

According to Fray Gabriel Téllez (better known as Tirso de Molina) in his *History of the Mercedarian Order*, the original monastery gradually became derelict, so that by the mid-16th century it could no longer accommodate the monks. This period saw the first attempts, particularly on the part of Fray Juan Bernal, to renovate the old building. However, no true progress was made until the early 17th century (with the Order by then led by the Sevillian

ROOM V. THE CHURCH.

monk Alonso de Monroy), when the city's chief architect and master builder, Juan de Oviedo y la Bandera, was commissioned to design a new monastery. The result, except for a few small alterations made in the 18th century, is the building as it stands today.

One of the finest examples of Andalusian late-Mannerist architecture, the monastery displays a structure with a new form of spatial arrangement — around three cloistered courtyards — whose various levels are connected by a large Imperial staircase. Known as the *Patio del Aljibe* or "Well Courtyard", the first courtyard rises in three levels with alternating enclosed spaces and open galleries of delicate columns. The first floor houses the Library. The lower gallery is adorned with rich panels of tiling dating from the 16th to the 18th century which came from secularized monasteries and were installed after 1868. Of these, particularly important are the *Evangelist* panel, from the workshop of Francisco Niculoso Pisano and dated *c.* 1525, and the large *Our Lady of the Rosary* panel, made in 1577 by Cristóbal de Augusta for the Convent of Madre de Dios in Seville. Beneath the courtyard is a deep well — hence its name — with a beautifully decorated 17th-century stone curb.

The second courtyard, the *Patio de los Bojes* or "Box-tree Courtyard", is one of the building's finest examples of Mannerist architecture. It boasts a wide variety of ornamentation that includes galleries of Tuscan arches and columns (with capitals surmounted with cymatia) supporting a second floor displaying cornices, brick pilasters and decorated balconies. An area of privacy for the monks and of recreation for the novices, it was adorned with canvases painted by Zurbarán in 1628. It presently houses various works of art, one being a Renaissance portal

carved by the Genoese Egidio de Grandia between 1510 and 1512 for the private chapel at La Calahorra Castle (Granada). This area also contains panels and murals of Triana tiling, including those of the *Immaculate Conception* (*c.* 1650) and *Our Lady of Santa Maria del Popolo* (*c.* 1670), and a predella dedicated to Seville's female patron saints, Justa and Rufina, and painted by Hernando de Valladares at his Triana workshop *c.* 1600.

The last courtyard, the *Claustro Mayor* or "Great Cloister", which was completed before 1615, was built in line with the new liturgy of the Counter-Reformation and the great monastic processions. Its garden is delightful, as are its low galleries with arches of elegant proportions supported by coupled columns which run the length of a tall continuous plinth. These galleries have retained most of their original tiling (also made by Hernando de Valladares *c.* 1620) whose most interesting feature is a number of small pilasters adorned with caryatids and other figures. The enclosed, balconied upper floor was modified in the 18th century by the local architect Leonardo de Figueroa, who added the coupled Ionic pilasters of pressed brick. Adorned after the beginning of the 17th century with canvases by Pacheco and Vázquez and with small chapels, it also displays a number of reliefs by Sevillian sculptors and a sundial designed by Juan de Oviedo in 1612 and decorated according to the *sgraffito* technique.

Other areas of special importance in the original ground-floor layout of the monastery which have been adapted are: to the south and adjacent to the Patio de los Bojes, the great Refectory, now Room II, which is a large rectangular hall with a flat ceiling of thick beams resting on decorated double corbels; to the west, the De

ROOM II. THE REFECTORY.

Profundis Room, now Room IV; and, to the north, the church, which, despite its extremely simple structure was originally richly decorated and one of the largest of its kind in Seville. Built without side chapels, it consisted of a single section with double pilasters, a small transept, and a small sanctuary. The entrance, from the Calle de Bailén, was adorned with a monumental portal — which now frames the Museum's main entrance — carved in 1792 by Miguel de Quintana. The altarpieces were made by Francisco Dionisio and Gaspar de Ribas, while the rich fresco decoration was painted in the mid-18th century by the local artist Domingo Martínez. It also had a large ante-sacristy with a carved flat panelled ceiling divided in two. This room now serves as the Museum's temporary exhibitions room. When the original sacristy was destroyed by fire in 1810, its site became that of the *Patio de las Conchas* or "Courtyard of Shells".

Formerly occupied almost entirely by the monks' cells, the upper floor of the building is reached by means of the monumental Imperial staircase, built in 1612 after plans by Juan de Oviedo. The staircase is the architectural heart of the building, for the whole arrangement of this national monument is laid out around it. Its position away from the monastery entrances underlines its function as a private area in the everyday life of the monastery. With a double splay at its upper and lower levels, it consists structurally of two highly decorated sections, all being surmounted by an octagonal dome resting on squinches. The dome's rich stucco decoration, which displays very interesting Marian iconography, is a fine example of Mannerist ornamentation and aesthetics.

Enrique Pareja López
Director

Mediaeval Art

• Room I •

Mediaeval Spanish Art

The Sevillian School

Mediaeval Sevillian Sculpture

Anonymous. Juan Sánchez de Castro's circle. *Panel Paintings of the Military Orders* (c. 1480).

• Room I

One of the Museum's main attractions is its examples of the work of the Sevillian school, a considerably homogeneous movement which, in contrast with other Spanish schools, consistently produced works of high standard from the Middle Ages on. However, since the end of the 19th century, various legacies have enabled the Museum to assemble an interesting collection of work by various of these national schools.

Mediaeval Spanish Art

From the Zayas donation, the *Ascension* panels follow the style of the most famous exponent of International Gothic in Catalonia, the Catalan master Bernardo Martorell, while the *Virgin with Musical Angels*, which displays the continued prevalence of Italian influence on the Valencia school, is after the style of the Valencian painter Almonacid. From the González Abreu legacy, the excellent *Jacob's Dream* has recently been attributed to a follower of the Burgos painter Diego de la Cruz, while the *Christ with the Virgin and St Mary Magdalene* triptych is from the circle of Loteta, an Aragonese artist also associated with the International Gothic style. The style of *St John the Baptist*, a donation by Diego Angulo, closely resembles that of the Cordovan Bartolomé Bermejo, a major exponent of the Hispanic-Flemish style prevalent in the second half of the 15th century.

ANONYMOUS. JUAN SÁNCHEZ DE CASTRO'S CIRCLE. *PANEL PAINTINGS OF THE MILITARY ORDERS* (c. 1480).

Sculpture is represented through images of polychrome wood by masters of the Castilian school. The iconography of the *Virgin and Child* is similar to that of the *Theokotos* of Byzantium, depicting a seated Virgin Mary with the Child among her skirts. The *Christ Crucified*, in which the dead Christ is crowned, displays iconographic models of Central European origin.

The Sevillian School

The Sevillian school appeared some time after the reconquest of the city by Ferdinand III in 1248, the first known examples of its production dating from the 14th century. However, paintings which were signed or by artists of renown did not begin to appear until the 15th century, the date of the Museum's earliest exhibits of this kind.

From the outset the school displayed certain features which, with the passing of the centuries (and times of splendour often followed by periods of lesser creative power) were to endow it with a distinctive character of its own.

As in the rest of Spain and Europe in the first half of the 15th century, local art tended to be dominated by a combination of Flemish influences. In Seville this coincided with a period of great artistic vitality and strong economic development.

The most prominent figure in mediaeval Sevillian painting is Juan Sánchez de Castro, who worked in the city in the second half of the century. Although the Museum does not possess

ANONYMOUS. JUAN SÁNCHEZ DE CASTRO'S CIRCLE. *THE PASSION OF CHRIST ALTARPIECE* (c. 1415).

any of his paintings, it does exhibit works by artists influenced by his style.

Particularly important among these is a set of four panels of pairs of saints originally from the old high altarpiece in the Church of San Benito de Calatrava in Seville. The saints portrayed are *S.S. Jerome and Anthony of Padua, Andrew and John the Baptist, Antonio Abbot and Christopher* and *Catherine and Sebastian*. The rich decoration in these paintings is revealed in the garments, the gold backgrounds, and the tracery paving.

In the mid-17th century these panels were replaced by others painted by Valdés Leal. They

remained in storage until 1908, when they were transferred on permanent loan to the Museum by the Military Orders.

Also from the circle of painters influenced by Juan Sánchez de Castro is the anonymous *Passion of Christ Altarpiece*, which came from the Montpensier Collection. Here the central *Calvary* panel is flanked on the left by a *Prayer in the Garden* and a *Flagellation* and on the right by a *Crucifixion* and a *Pietà* (in which St Francis is depicted receiving the stigmata). These highly expressive paintings with detailed depictions of secondary episodes in the background are typical of the Flemish-influenced works of the times.

The influence of another Sevillian artist, Juan Hispalense, who worked in Castile for most of his life, is reflected in *St Michael the Archangel.*

Mediaeval Sevillian Sculpture

The origin of mediaeval Sevillian sculpture lies in the second half of the 15th century and is linked to a French image-maker who castianized his name to Lorenzo Mercadante de Bretaña.

According to records, Mercadante de Bretaña was active in Seville between 1454 and 1468 and enjoyed a great deal of success with the new Burgundian style. The result was one type of painting filled with a predominantly northern European devotional quality and another with the naturalism and meticulous attention to detail so typical of the Flemish school. Mercadante de Bretaña worked with alabaster and clay, using the latter for the *Nativity* and *Baptism* entrances to Seville Cathedral, his most popular works. His influence on Sevillian late-Gothic sculpture was considerable and his principal follower was Pedro Millán.

Millán is the first local image-maker mentioned in the records (1487-1506). Most of his works are of terracotta and normally bear his signature. One of his finest pieces and the oldest of its kind in Spain, his *Entombment of Christ* reveals the influence of the French and Italian pioneers in a theme that was to become so popular in Europe in the mid-15th century. Millán's signature – *P MILLAN IMA* – appears in Gothic script among symbols of the Passion and thistle flowers on the front of the sarcophagus pedestal.

PEDRO MILLÁN. *THE ENTOMBMENT OF CHRIST.* (c. 1490).

The 16th Century. The Renaissance and Mannerism

• ROOM II

For Seville, the 16th century brought strong economic development due to a boom in trade with the Americas and the rest of Europe. A higher demand for works of art and the arrival of foreign artists, particularly from Flanders and Italy, prompted a process of renewal in art. The harmonious blending of the two styles led to the appearance of a novel form of art of high technical perfection in which a number of local artists soon excelled.

The Flemish School

One example of that new cultural environment is the Museum's collection of Flemish paintings, most of which were acquired in the wake of the Disentailment Act and to a lesser degree through private donations. Interesting among these are a number of works associated with the style of lesser masters like Vicente Sellaer, Pieter Pourbus and the *Maestros* of Las Medias Figuras and El Papagayo. With his *Virgin and Child* (c. 1550) Guillaume Benson (Bruges?-Middelburg 1574) painted a highly successful prototype for numerous variations on a theme established by Roger van der Weyden, a painter of the previous generation.

By Marcello Coffermans, a master of the School of Antwerp from 1549, is a highly symmetrical and intimist *Virgin and Child* (c. 1560). Also attributed to Coffermans, the *Annunciation and Visitation Diptych* (c. 1570) was bequeathed to the Museum in the González Abreu legacy.

Although Peter Aertsen (Amsterdam 1508-1575) is known mainly for his large *bodegones*,

GUILLAUME BENSON.
VIRGIN AND CHILD (c. 1550).

he also painted religious themes. The *Assumption and Coronation of the Virgin* displays such typical features of his work as the stylization of figures, angels with wings similar to those of butterflies, and landscapes full of rich colour.

Also exhibited in this room are two works in the late 16th century Mannerist style by prominent members of the School of Antwerp: Frans Francken I and Maarten de Vos. In the 16th and 17th centuries, Antwerp was not only the greatest centre of art in the Low Countries but one of the most important in Europe. Italian Renaissance forms reached the city rapidly after 1500, but the deep-rooted tradition of Flemish painting made the incorporation of novelties a slow, gradual process. However, by the end of the 16th century, the refined, international art of Mannerism had become highly popular at the European courts.

Maarten de Vos.
The Last Judgement (1570).

Frans Francken I.
The Calvary Triptych (c. 1585).

By Frans Francken I (Herenthal 1542-Antwerp 1616) the Museum possesses a splendid triptych which came originally from the Hospital de las Bubas in Seville and is considered one of the most important of its kind in Spain. The central panel is a *Calvary* (*c.* 1585) with a scene from the *Road to Calvary* on its left and a *Descent from the Cross* on its right. On the backs of these side panels are a *Virgin and Child* and a *St Bernard*.

Until only recently this work was attributed to Frans Floris, an artist regarded as a pioneer of the Renaissance in northern Europe. Floris was a representative of the "Romanist" trend and the influence of his monumental idealized figures painted in a wide range of colours is also evident in the work of his follower Frans Francken.

Maarten de Vos (Antwerp 1532-1604) was the most relevant Antwerp artist of the second half of the 16th century. Three paintings of his came to the Museum from an altarpiece in the Monastery of San Agustín with the enforcement of the Disentailment Act. Signed and dated in 1570, the central panel is a *Last Judgement*, while the side panels portray *St Augustine* and *St Francis*. These works illustrate the harmonious combination of Italian and School of Antwerp styles that is characteristic of this painter's work. De Vos spent six years in Italy, where he enriched his palette with a wide variety of typically Venetian tones. He was especially skilful in the composition and execution of scenes containing a variety of expressive figures and his works, which became popular all over Europe thanks to the art of engraving, served as a source of inspiration for a large number of artists, among these Sevillians like Alonso Vázquez.

LUCAS CRANACH.
CALVARY (1538).

In a scene on two planes illustrating the Earthly and the Celestial, de Vos's *Last Judgement* depicts the joyous resurrection of the blessed, while the condemned, horrified and gesticulating, are dragged off to hell.

The German School

From another Central European circle – the German school – Lucas Cranach (Cranach 1472-Weimar 1553) is regarded as second only to the great German Renaissance painter Albrecht Dürer. The Museum possesses an excellent *Calvary* signed and dated by Cranach in 1538, when he was in his

(OPPOSITE) DOMENICOS TEOTOCOPULOS, EL GRECO.
JORGE MANUEL THEOTOCOPOULOS (*c.* 1600-1605).

Anonymous Sevillian.
Our Lady of La Antigua (c. 1500).

artistic prime. It depicts Christ on the cross between the two thieves, and the centurion on horseback attired as a 16th-century knight. A number of features typical of Cranach's stylistic maturity – flat surfaces as bright and polished as enamel and sharply-contoured figures against a dark background – are evident in this painting.

The Spanish School

In sharp contrast with a small number of pictures by artists such as *Maestros* Bonnat and Cueza (which, though not without interest, are of lesser importance) this room displays exceptional works by one of the greatest representatives of all Spanish painting – Domenicos Theotocopoulos, *El Greco* (Candia, Crete 1541-Toledo 1614). El Greco acquired his unique style in Italy but did not reach full stylistic maturity until his return to Spain. Typical of his work are vertical compositions, elongated figures and ranges of cold colours through which forms are broken down with brilliant light. It is in his portraits that the most realistic facet of his style is revealed. In his depiction of his son *Jorge Manuel Theotocopoulos* (c. 1600-1605), he focused not only on his model's hands but also on the head, emphasizing it with a white ruff against a greenish neutral background. The elegant figure is depicted with the professional attributes of a painter, although Jorge Manuel was to be more renowned as an architect.

The Sevillian School

Alejo Fernández (c. 1475-Seville 1545) is regarded as the artist who introduced the spirit of the Renaissance into Sevillian painting. Of German origin, he is known to have lived in Córdoba in the late 15th century, having taken his Spanish wife's surname. By 1508 he had settled in Seville and was soon working on commissions for a number of important clients, including the Cathedral chapter. His style reveals a mixture of Flemish and Italian influence that is clearly distinguishable in his lovely

(Opposite) Alejo Fernández.
The Annunciation (c. 1508).

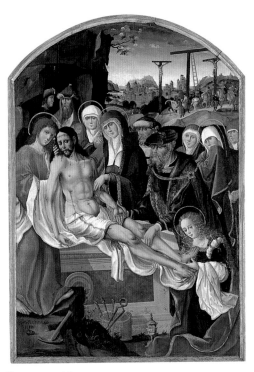

CRISTÓBAL DE MORALES
THE ENTOMBMENT OF CHRIST (*c.* 1525).

Annunciation (*c.* 1508) panel. Here such typically Italian features as emphasis on perspective, symmetry and Classical architecture combine with the painstaking attention to detail so characteristic of the Flemish painters.

The presence in Seville of a contemporary of Fernández's, Cristóbal de Morales, is documented between 1509 and 1526. The Museum possesses his only known signed work, an *Entombment of Christ* (*c.* 1525) originally from the Convent of Madre de Dios.

While Fernández was responsible for bringing the Quattrocento style to the Sevillian School, it was a Flemish painter, Pieter de Kempener (Brussels 1503-*c.* 1580) who in the second third of the 16th century introduced the Cinquecento

or Romanist style. A Humanist, architect and sculptor, Kempener became the most famous painter of the Sevillian Renaissance thanks to paintings like his *Descent from the Cross*, which is now in the Cathedral. Another prominent painter of Flemish origin was Hernando Sturmio (Zierikzee, Holland *c.* 1515-Seville 1556), who painted the great *Evangelists* altarpiece in the Cathedral.

No record of the work of celebrated local artists exists until that of the first great Seville-born artist Luis de Vargas (Seville *c.* 1505-1567) in the second half of the century. By Vargas the Museum possesses a *Purification* on board (*c.* 1560) whose figures and architectural backgrounds reveal the painter's Italian training within the large circle of Raphael followers.

This Flemish and Italian-influenced style predominant in the second third of the 16th century was also developed by Pedro de Villegas Marmolejo (Seville 1519-1596), a Humanist closely associated with the city's intellectual circles whose best-known work is the Cathedral's *Visitation Altarpiece*. This room contains two of his panels for a small organ depicting *S.S. Thomas Aquinas and Catherine of Siena* and the *Holy Family with the Infant St John the Baptist* (*c.* 1550).

Important among the last generation of Sevillian artists of the 16th century who continued to work in the rigid Mannerist style – a style whose disappearance at the beginning of the 17th century was to prompt a process of renewal – were Alonso Vázquez and Vasco Pereira.

Renaissance Sculpture

Spanish sculpture experienced a period of great splendour in the 16th century. The early

LUIS DE VARGAS. *THE PURIFICATION* (c. 1560).

Roque Balduque.
Our Lady of The Rosary (h.1550).

decades saw the arrival of the new aesthetics of the Renaissance – a process favoured by Spain's close political ties with Italy, economic prosperity and a Spanish aristocracy that had embraced Humanism. Works of art were imported from Italy, and northern European and Italian artists who had assimilated the new Renaissance ways came to work in Spain.

Various artistic tendencies coexisted in Seville during the early decades of the century. The new Renaissance ways had reached Seville but the Gothic style still survived in the sculptural ornamentation of façades, altarpieces, choir stalls and imagery. Particularly important among the numerous craftsmen who came to Seville from other parts of Spain to work on the Cathedral were Miguel Perrín, Diego de Riaño (a Santander sculptor commissioned for the work

on the Town Hall) and Jorge Fernández, who collaborated on the high altarpiece in the Cathedral.

Roche de Balduque (Bois-le-Duc, Brabant ?- Seville 1561), was a Flemish sculptor whose presence is documented in Seville between 1534 and 1561, the year of his death. His production can be divided into two types – single images and sculptures and reliefs for altarpieces. After working on the high altarpiece in the Cathedral, he was engaged in a number of other projects, including those at the churches of San Lorenzo in Seville and Santo Domingo in Jerez, where he combined features of the Gothic naturalism typical of Flanders with the novelties of the Italian Renaissance. Although he engaged in all the sculptural genres, he specialized in Marian images, receiving numerous commissions from parish churches. His extremely delicate *Our Lady of the Rosary* (*c.* 1560), which dates from his mature years, was donated to the Museum by González Abreu. Dating from the earliest times, the iconographic theme of Mary as the mother of Jesus in Christian art became especially popular in the 15th century thanks to engravings and prints, and reached a high degree of development in the 16th century. This representation displays the half moon at the Virgin Mary's feet and the tabernacle on her chest, but a unique feature of the sculpture is that she holds the Child in her arms.

– The Italian Renaissance: Pietro Torrigiani

The initial impact of Renaissance art in Spain caused by the imported works of artists like Domenico Fancelli or Rosso and Francesco Fiorentino was of Quattrocento origin and

Pietro Torrigiani. *St Jerome* (1525).

MARTÍNEZ MONTAÑÉS.
St John Before the Latin Gate.

arrived somewhat belatedly. One exception was the work of Torrigiani, which brought the advanced forms of the High Renaissance then prevalent in Italy to Spain.

Pietro Torrigiani (Florence 1472-Seville 1528) was a companion and rival of Michelangelo's at the "De'Medici Garden" school. After an eventful life, he reached Seville in 1522, and was commissioned with two works for the Monastery of San Jerónimo de Buenavista – *St Jerome* and *Our Lady of Bethlehem* (both dated 1525) – which came to the Museum with disentailment. The Classical forms of the great Cinquecento masters as seen in these two works were so novel that it was several generations before they had been

assimilated by local artists. *Our Lady of Bethlehem* is a clear example of a form of Classicism and serenity greatly in keeping with geometric abstraction. Torrigiani's statue of *St Jerome* not only influenced sculptors in Andalusia but also in Italy, its iconography serving as a model for and constant inspiration to Spanish artists. The highly expressive head and splendid nude study in this full-size statue are quite startling and demonstrate his deep knowledge of sculpting from life. It was made in baked clay, a technique very popular in Italy and incorporated into the tradition of Sevillian sculpture in the 15th century.

• Room III

Renaissance and Early-Baroque Altarpieces

The altarpiece is one of Spain's greatest contributions to the history of art. The Catholic church used images to educate and influence the faithful and throughout the Renaissance filled chapels with scenes illustrating religious themes. Given its structure, the altarpiece was highly appropriate for experimentation and the 16th century saw the appearance of a wide range of different types. The materials used in making altarpieces were various: in Italy the use of marble and bronze was widespread, whereas in Spain the material *par excellence* was wood as it was believed to offer a higher degree of expressive potential. Once finished, the carved piece was coloured and gilded, leading on many occasions to collaboration between sculptor and painter.

Prominent among the large circle of followers and collaborators of the Flemish sculptor Roche de Balduque was Jean Girault (Flanders?-Seville

VIEW OF ROOM III.

1574), who accentuated northern European features through dramatic, angular figures betraying an incorrect assimilation of Renaissance principles. Girault's *Redemption Altarpiece* (1562), whose cedarwood reliefs are burnished with gold, came to the Museum from the Convent of Santa Catalina de Aracena in Huelva.

In the second half of the 16th century Sevillian sculpture became definitively consolidated through the Castilian masters acquainted with Cinquecento art who had brought Berruguete's expressive forms to Spain. Prominent among those who introduced the new Italian spirit were Isidro de Villoldo and Juan Bautista Vázquez the Elder. Vázquez headed the Sevillian School and was joined by such artists as Diego de Velasco, Miguel Adán, Gaspar del Águila, Juan Marín and Diego Pesquera. Equally important in this respect was Jerónimo Hernández (*c.* 1540-1586), whose workshop became a school for the last generation of artists with early-Baroque styles who included Vázquez the Younger, Marcos Cabrera, Núñez Delgado, Juan de Oviedo the Younger and Andrés de Ocampo.

Miguel Adán (Pinto, Madrid 1532-Seville 1610) is best known for his altarpieces. The Museum possesses six of the reliefs he made for the *St John the Baptist Altarpiece* (1592-1594) at the Convent of Las Dueñas in Seville. With the Disentailment Act, this collection, which was painted by Vasco Pereira, was divided up between the Cathedral, the Church of Santa María and the Museum.

The production of Andrés de Ocampo (Villacarrillo, Jaén 1550?-Seville 1623), another sculptor who received his training at Jerónimo Hernández's workshop, is well documented. Typical of his style are well-balanced volumes, attention to detail reminiscent of Baroque trends, and suggestions of the same Classicism which characterized Hernández's work. Ocampo's *High Altarpiece* from the Convent of Las Dueñas in Seville (1586-92) contains a number of scenes illustrative of the transition to Baroque.

In the 17th century, Baroque trends became prevalent in sculpture thanks to Juan Martínez Montañés (Alcalá la Real 1568-Seville 1649) and Juan de Mesa (Córdoba 1583-Seville 1627). In the diocese of Seville Montañés employed a highly personal style of altarpiece composition based on the principles of Serlio and Palladio.

Together with the paintings of Francisco Varela (1580/85-Seville 1645) this room displays the relief from the *St John the Evangelist Altarpiece* (1638) made for Convent of Las Monjas de Pasión in Seville.

Francisco Pacheco and the Painting of His Age

Two movements – Mannerism and Naturalism – converged in Sevillian painting during the early decades of the 17th century. The former perpetuated the tradition of the painters of the late 16th century through rigid, schematic forms of expression shunning any kind of change, while the latter represented renewal, as based on a direct, narrative language in pursuit of a transcription of life. Francisco Pacheco and Juan de Roelas were the most representative exponents of the confrontation between these two movements.

More famous as Velázquez's father-in-law and for his treatise *El Arte de la Pintura* ("The Art of Painting") than for his artistic abilities, Francisco Pacheco (Sanlúcar de Barrameda 1564-Seville

FRANCISCO PACHECO. *THE MYSTIC MARRIAGE OF ST AGNES* (1628).

Francisco Pacheco. *Personages in an Attitude of Prayer* (c. 1630).

1644) represents the Mannerist tradition. The Museum possesses a large enough number of his works to allow an appreciation of his style, the first examples being among the pictures he painted with Alonso Vázquez for the Monastery of La Merced in Seville, which now houses this Museum.

His series of paintings from the *St John the Baptist Altarpiece* in the Convent of Las Monjas de Pasión, Seville, dates from around 1610. Here a statue of the saint in a niche was flanked by paintings of St Francis and St Dominic, while the predella displayed portraits of the four evangelists.

In the course of the same decade Pacheco painted another series for the Church of San Esteban, in all likelihood for an altarpiece. At the centre *St John the Evangelist and the Virgin* flanked a statue of *Christ on the Cross*, while at the sides were six images of saints.

Pacheco came into his artistic prime in 1615, and as a Humanist and scholar, a writer and theoretician, a collector, director of the Seville Academy and Inquisition censor, was for many years Seville's most famous painter. Between 1615 and 1620 he painted a splendid *St Francis* full of his characteristic simplicity and expressive sobriety for the monastery dedicated to the saint in Alcalá de Guadaira.

From a somewhat later period (1628) is one of his most beautiful works, *The Mystic Marriage of St Agnes*, which combines a certain capacity for abstraction with a gentle intimist expressiveness.

In the face of the new naturalism advanced by painters like Roelas, Herrera the Elder and Zurbarán, around 1625 interest in Pacheco's work began to wane.

His most important commission thereafter was the high altarpiece paintings (now lost) for

FRANCISCO PACHECO. *PERSONAGES IN AN ATTITUDE OF PRAYER* (c. 1630).

the Convent of La Pasión church in Seville. Painted around 1630, these consisted of *Prayer in the Garden, The Flagellation, The Crowning with Thorns* and *Christ Carrying the Cross*. In each case *tenebrism* was stressed with stylistically regressive features more typical of reformed Mannerism than of the art of Pacheco's time. Also from this period are his portraits of an *Elderly Lady and Gentleman* and a *Young Lady and Gentleman* for the predella of the Monastery of El Santo Angel altarpiece.

The Sevillian Period in the Work of Diego Velázquez and Alonso Cano

Two of the most important representatives of 16th-century Spanish art – Diego Velázquez and Alonso Cano – received their early training under Pacheco. Their interest in naturalism and the use of light plus the presence of Flemish and Italian painting in Seville which responded to that interpretation of naturalism called *tenebrism*, was to mark the beginning of their careers.

Diego Rodríguez de Silva y Velázquez (Seville 1599-Madrid 1660) first studied under Herrera the Elder, but soon transferred to Pacheco's workshop. He married Pacheco's daughter Juana in 1617.

During his period in Seville Velázquez found a way of expressing his interest in *chiaroscuro* and naturalism through genre painting and *bodegones* with figures – fields with precedents in both Flemish and Italian painting. With his exceptional mastery of drawing and a dark colour range which served to emphasize the effects of *tenebrism*, Velázquez achieved an extraordinary

39

Alonso Cano.
St Francis Borgia (1624).

degrêe of realism in his scenes of everyday life. During his Sevillian period he practised two other genres – religious painting and portraiture – also with highly realistic results. A fine example of his great skill as a portraitist is his painting of *Don Cristóbal Suárez de Riberas* (1620), a Sevillian clergyman and founder of a brotherhood devoted to St Hermenegild, whose emblem is included in the top left-hand corner of the picture.

Aware of his exceptional abilities as an artist, Velázquez travelled to Madrid in 1622 in pursuit of a goal common to all painters of that period – an appointment as "Painter to the King". This he achieved at the end of 1623 thanks to the help of Gaspar de Guzmán, Count of Olivares, and the acceptance of his first portrait of Philip IV. Velázquez and his family then moved to Madrid, bringing his Sevillian period to an end.

When Alonso Cano (Granada 1601-1667) entered Pacheco's workshop in 1616, Velázquez had recently completed his period of apprenticeship. It is highly likely that he also worked in Martínez Montañés's workshop, devoting the rest of his life to painting, sculpture and architectural design.

In *St Francis Borgia* (1624), one of his first known works, his use of accurate modelling and contrasts of light to emphasize expressive drama reflect Pacheco's influence. Also by Cano is *The Souls in Purgatory* (1636), a painting on board from the predella of an altarpiece in the Monastery of Monte Sión, Seville.

• Room IV

Painting of the Last Third of the 16th Century: Alonso Vázquez

Besides Pacheco, Alonso Vázquez and the Portuguese Vasco Pereira were other very relevant members of the last generation of Mannerist artists who were active in Seville in the 16th century.

Vázquez (*c.* 1540?-Mexico *c.* 1608) is known to have lived and worked in Seville from 1588. In 1603 he left Spain for Mexico, where he remained until 1608, deeply influencing the Mexican painting of the first half of the 17th century.

Vázquez's style is full of that mixture of Flemish and Italian elements which characterizes Sevillian painting until well into the 17th centu-

(Opposite) Diego Velázquez.
Don Cristóbal Suárez de Ribera (1620).

Alonso Vázquez. *The Last Supper* (1588).

ry. Faithful to the principles of late Mannerism, his painting experienced little development and displays a repetition of similar compositional forms and figures. This was largely due to the tastes of a clientele which required compositions always of the same kind as well as the widespread use within the Sevillian School of the engravings of masters of previous generations like the Flemish artist Maarten de Vos.

This room contains Vázquez's first known work, *The Last Supper*, which he painted for the La Cartuja refectory in 1588. Based on a number of engravings, it displays naturalist elements

in the chinaware and food together with features of conventional contemporary Mannerism such as artificial colours and figures with sharply-defined bodies and emphatic gestures. From around 1603 and recently attributed to Vázquez is an elegant *Virgin of the Immaculate Conception*, which he was subsequently to make an almost exact copy of for the Hospital de la Purísima Concepción in Mexico. This too is based on an engraving, but Vázquez concentrated on elements identifying Mary as a woman of the Apocalypse and included other features in the landscape emphasizing her purity.

ALONSO VÁZQUEZ. *ST PETER NOLASCO REDEEMING CAPTIVES* (1601).

In 1600 Vázquez and Francisco Pacheco were commissioned by the Monastery of La Merced to paint a series of paintings for the main cloister extolling the history of the Order and its most illustrious members. The Order of Our Lady of Mercy was founded in the Middle Ages to redeem Christians from the Moors and Mediterranean pirates. According to tradition, the first Mercedarian monastery in Seville was founded by St Peter Nolasco on land ceded by Ferdinand III after his conquest of Seville in 1248. At the beginning of the 17th century, when Fray Alonso de Monroy was General of the Order, the building was completely renovated in order to adapt it to the requirements of the Counter-Reformation. The architect and sculptor Juan de Oviedo y de la Bandera was commissioned to direct the major construction work carried out on the building and the most noteworthy local artists to adorn it. Consequently, when the Disentailment Act was passed, it was already well suited to its new purpose as a provincial museum.

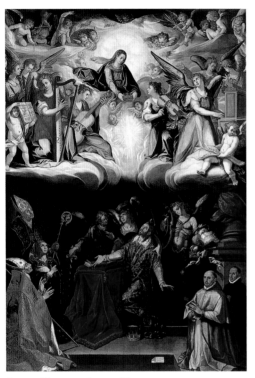

ALONSO VÁZQUEZ - JUAN DE UCEDA.
THE PASSING OF ST HERMENEGILD (1603).

As Francisco Pacheco recorded in *El Arte de la Pintura* ("The Art of Painting"), he and Alonso Vázquez received the commission for the decoration of the monastery's main cloister in 1600. The series of pictures they painted – only four of which have remained in the Museum – told the story of the Order and its most illustrious members, the founders Saints Peter Nolasco and Raymund Nonnatus. Vázquez's paintings depict the transaction of a redemption and St Peter Nolasco's interview with James I. Both canvases reflect Vázquez's style, the firmness of his lines and the gravity of his monumental figures. Pacheco painted the scene of the redemption of captives with St Peter helped aboard a boat, and the appearance

of the Virgin Mary to St Raymund Nonnatus. Both paintings suffer from a certain rigidity and lack of expressiveness betraying the use of engravings, and the persistence of Mannerism in Pacheco's style.

Another example of the continuation of the tradition of the previous century is a painting for which Vázquez received the original commission from the local Hospital of San Hermenegildo in 1603. Vázquez left Spain for Mexico that year and the painting, which was to be the focal point of an altarpiece illustrating *The Passing of St Hermenegild*, was completed by Juan de Uceda. The preparation and general composition are due to Vázquez, who also painted the lower section, in which St Hermenegild, accompanied by King Recared and S.S. Isidore and Leander, is comforted by angels. The physical characteristics of some of the angels in the upper section are also typical of Vázquez's style.

Sculpture of the Turn of the 16th Century: Small Masterpieces

In this room, sculpture illustrates two very popular iconographic themes of Spanish Baroque: heads of decapitated saints and the Christ Child.

Signed and dated 1591, the *Head of St John the Baptist* was carved by Gaspar Núñez Delgado, who lived and worked in Seville from 1576 to 1606. A sculptor active at the turn of the 16th century, Núñez was a master of all materials and techniques and produced splendid works of ivory, clay and polychrome wood.

The iconography used in this type of sculpture spread through Seville after the publication of an illustration on the theme by the German Jacob

Gaspar Núñez Delgado. *Head of St John the Baptist* (1591).

Cromberger in the *Life of Christ Altarpiece*, a book written by the Sevillian Carthusian monk Juan de Padilla. Núñez Delgado's work is doubly interesting in that it served as a model for subsequent Baroque images and was the precursor of the typically Sevillian manner of portraying the hair – tousled with a lock hanging over the forehead.

After Jerónimo Hernández and his disciple Núñez Delgado, the most prominent figure in the first generation of Baroque sculptors was Juan Martínez Montañés (Alcalá la Real 1568-Seville 1649). Martínez Montañés's Renaissance heritage is evident in the balance and compositional arrangement of his works, but a vibrant restlessness betrays the nascent expressiveness of Baroque art.

Montañés created a type of infant Jesus sculpture of extreme sensitivity, one fine example, from the Sacrarium of Seville Cathedral, being *The Christ Child Giving His Blessing*. This iconographic theme, which originated in early-Christian times, continued to be commonly used in Gothic and early-Renaissance art and became very popular in Baroque art. Particularly famous are the "Infants" of Jerónimo Hernández, Diego Velasco, Juan de Oviedo and, above all, of Montañés.

The success of Montañés's figures gave rise to numerous versions from his own workshop, noteworthy examples being those of Juan de Mesa. Cheaper clay and polychrome lead versions made the theme even more popular, particularly for private devotion.

The 17th Century. Naturalism and Baroque

- Rooms III to VIII.
  Spanish Baroque Painting

The most important works in the Museum's collection were executed by the great masters of the 17th century, particularly those of the Sevillian school. Other national centres of art like Madrid and Toledo are also represented here together with works by such exceptional artists as José de Ribera. An interesting collection of European Baroque painting – basically Flemish and Italian – brings this section on 17th-century art to an end.

The Sevillian School

Seville experienced an economic boom in the second half of the 16th century and became the greatest Western capital. Art production also reaped the benefits of trade with Europe and the Americas, leading to the import of works of art from abroad and commissions which attracted many foreign artists. This burgeoning of trade and art reached a peak in the reign of Philip III (1598-1621) and laid the foundations for the artistic splendour of Philip IV's reign (1621-1665).

In the early decades of the 17th century Seville continued to be Spain's greatest city and the immensely rich home of trade with the Americas. However, the first symptoms of economic decline appeared in the late 16th century and from 1640 the city suffered a succession of adversities and disasters which led to economic stagnation, while the population was decimated by a series of epidemics and natural catastrophes. These adverse circumstances plus the misfortunes of the populace led to a general change in mentality and intensified feelings of piety which permeated all Sevillian society, prompting higher demand for religious works. By this time there was a great deal of private and corporate patronage of the arts and Seville's workshops were producing works for both the busy domestic market and export to the Americas.

However, the principal patron of the arts in the 17th century was the Church. During the economic boom of the previous century it had commissioned large buildings which were now in need of adornment with paintings and sculptures. These works of art were either paid for directly by the Church or by aristocrats who subsequently donated them to parish churches, monasteries and convents.

– Sevillian Painting of the First Third of the 17th century (Rooms V and VI)

Much of the tradition of the 16th-century Seville school lived on in the 17th-century school. However, it was the Mannerist tendency which, decades later, facilitated the development of the great 17th-century Sevillian painting through the advent of Baroque freedom. Of the first generation of artists, Francisco Pacheco best represents the persistence of tradition and Juan de Roelas the naturalist renewal based on a direct, narrative form of language that was finally to prevail.

*Juan de Roelas (Seville 1558/60-Olivares 1621)
(Rooms III and V)*

Juan de Roelas introduced the direct observation of nature and its colours, types and details

(Opposite) Juan de Roelas.
The Martyrdom of St Andrew (c. 1610).

Juan de Roelas.
St Anne Teaching the Virgin to Read (*c.* 1615).

to the Sevillian school. On a journey to Italy he saw the colour of Venetian art and on his return to Seville brought a palette of warm, golden tones and a type of large-format altar painting typical of the Counter-Reformation which was commonly used to illustrate two very different planes – the Earthly and the Celestial. A fine example of this is his most important work in the Museum, *The Martyrdom of St Andrew* (*c.* 1610), a monumental composition executed with a fluent technique focusing more on sumptuous, vibrant colour than on line. In a highly emotive scene the saint's transcendental experience is contrasted with the boisterousness of the spectators.

The Coming of the Holy Spirit (*c.* 1615) is another example of the monumental type of work which made such a deep impression on the Seville society of the times by combining celestial apotheosis with details from everyday life through portraiture.

Such interest in the everyday is also seen in the intimist depiction of *St Anne Teaching The Virgin to Read* (*c.* 1615), while *The Way to Calvary* (*c.* 1620) is a scene of high drama.

– The First Generation of Artists
   (Rooms III, IV and V)

Particularly important among the first generation of artists in Seville who, although trained in Mannerism, ultimately embraced naturalism, was Antonio Mohedano (Antequera 1561-1626). Of the small number of paintings produced by him the Museum possesses *The Holy Family* (*c.* 1610). The Museum also possesses the first known work of Juan de Uceda (Seville *c.* 1570-1631), who completed the *Passing of St Hermenegild* left unfinished by Alonso Vázquez on his departure for Mexico. An interesting fact about *The Trinity on Earth*, also by Uceda and signed and dated in 1623, is that it was painted for the Monastery of La Merced, which now houses this Museum. By Francisco Varela (1580/85-Seville 1645) are four panels originally from the *St John the Evangelist Altarpiece* (*c.* 1640) in the church of the Sevillian Convent of La Pasión. The focal point of the altarpiece was a relief of *St John the Evangelist* by Martínez Montañés flanked by paintings of *St Christopher* and *St Augustine* by Varela, with two predellas – depicting *St Catherine of Siena with St Lucy* and *St Catherine of Alexandria with St Teresa of Jesus* – below.

Juan del Castillo (Seville *c.* 1590-*c.* 1657/58) is known mainly as Murillo's teacher and for his

FRANCISCO HERRERA THE ELDER.
THE APOTHEOSIS OF ST HERMENEGILD (*c.* 1630).

between 1614 and 1631, and Miguel de Esquivel (Seville *c.* 1590/95-1621).

– The Second Generation of Artists:
The Triumph of Naturalism

Naturalism definitively superseded Mannerism with the second generation of painters of the 17th-century Sevillian school. Its greatest

FRANCISCO HERRERA THE ELDER.
VISION OF ST BASIL (*c.* 1638).

friendship with Alonso Cano. The Museum possesses his most important series of paintings (*c.* 1634-36), which came from the high altarpiece of the Monastery of Monte Sión in Seville. They reflect the maturity of his style, his competent draughtsmanship and also a gentle naturalism. Also by del Castillo are *St Dominic Scourging Himself* and *St Peter before Christ at the Column* (*c.* 1640, originally from the Capuchin monastery at Marchena) and the *Infant St John Attended by Angels* (*c.* 1640). Other prominent painters of this time were Paul Legot (Marche, Luxembourg 1598-Cadiz 1671), Juan Sánchez Cotán, whose work is documented in Seville

exponents in the second third of the century were Herrera the Elder and Zurbarán, whose styles – firm and expressive in Herrera's case, simple and intense in Zurbarán's – dominated the painting of the times.

Francisco Herrera the Elder (Seville c. 1590-Madrid 1654) (Room V)

Herrera the Elder was trained in the style imposed by painters like Pacheco but gradually abandoned Mannerism for naturalism.

The Museum possesses some of his best works, particularly important being *The Apotheosis of St Hermenegild* (*c.* 1620), painted for the Jesuit School of San Hermenegildo in Seville. The composition adheres to the strict lines of the previous generation, with volumes contrasted symmetrically and the scene divided into two sections representing Heaven and Earth. In Heaven and depicted along the lines laid down by Roelas is a triumphant St Hermenegild surrounded by angels, while on Earth St Isidore subdues Leovigild and St Leander protects Recared, the future king who will proclaim Spain a Catholic country at the Third Council of Toledo. The canvas displays the features typical of Herrera's mature style – fluent, energetic strokes forming highly individual faces and a colour range predominating in gold and black chestnut shades.

It appears that Herrera the Elder also painted *The Apotheosis of St Ignatius Loyola* (*c.* 1630) for the Jesuits, as the excellent study of the saint is clearly indicative of his masterful style. A *Virgin of the Immaculate Conception* from the same period (*c.* 1625-1630) was previously attributed to Roelas, but the precise lines and long brush-strokes sharply outlining the forms and the limited palette of iridescent colours all indicate that this is Herrera's work.

In 1638 Herrera received a commission for the high altarpiece paintings of the San Basilio Magno School church in Seville. Of the eighteen painted by him, nine – the central scene and eight portraits of saints of the Order – reached the Museum due to disentailment. The monumental *Vision of St Basil* is perhaps Herrera's best work. It depicts the saint's vision of heaven as he kneels before the altar contemplating Christ surrounded by the twelve Apostles in the revelation of the Glory of God. This multi-coloured composition was painted with a highly fluent technique full of expressiveness and energy which clearly anticipated the high Baroque style.

Francisco de Zurbarán (Fuente de Cantos, Badajoz 1598-Madrid 1664) (Rooms V, VI and X)

Francisco de Zurbarán was the most prominent Sevillian painter of the second third of the 17th century. Although born in Extremadura, he received his training in Seville, where he settled in 1626 and subsequently became the most favoured painter of the civil and religious institutions. During those brilliant years he painted unceasingly and was obliged to run a large workshop in order to cope with the huge demand for his religious works. His great success was due mainly to a sober, naturalist style, suffused with a deep sense of spirituality combining fervent passion and details of the everyday with the religious elements of Spanish monastic life.

The Museum possesses a number of fine paintings from his monastic cycles. Of the series of twenty-one portraits Zurbarán was commis-

FRANCISCO DE ZURBARÁN. *THE APOTHEOSIS OF ST THOMAS AQUINAS* (1631).

Francisco de Zurbarán.
The Blessed Enrique Susón (1636).

sioned to paint in 1626 for the Dominican Monastery of San Pablo in Seville, the Museum possesses three of his four Doctors of the Church – *St Ambrose, St Gregory* and *St Jerome.* The monumental figures display a feature that is constant in the whole of Zurbarán's work – masterful isolated figures endowed with compelling expressive power. Clothed in rich, surprisingly detailed liturgical vestments, they are portrayed against a dark background with a solemn sense of monumentality making their presence extremely immediate.

In 1628, after the great success of his series for the Dominicans, he received another important commission, on this occasion from the Monastery of La Merced Calzada, also in Seville, for twenty-two canvases on the life of the founder of the Mercedarian Order, St Peter Nolasco, and a number of portraits of its most illustrious friars. The Museum possesses two of these portraits, the Mercedarian friars *St Peter Pascual* and *St Carmelo*, in which Zurbarán was assisted by members of his workshop.

In 1631, Zurbarán painted what was probably his most ambitious project, *The Apotheosis of St Thomas Aquinas*, for the Dominican School of San Tomás Aquinas in Seville. As was customary he based it on engravings and again used the traditional division into two planes. On the left, in the lower half of the painting and kneeling around a bureau displaying the papal bull of the Order's foundation, is the school's founder, Fray Diego Deza, heading a group of Dominican friars, while on the right the Emperor Charles V, at the head of another group of figures, also kneels in prayer. The upper section is dominated by St Thomas himself flanked by the four Fathers of the Church, with, above them, the Holy Spirit, Christ and the Virgin on the left, and Saints Paul and Dominic on the right. One of Zurbarán's most complex works, this painting contains extremely monumental figures with highly naturalistic expressions in addition to various details revealing the painter's extraordinary skill in the depiction of his themes.

At around this time (*c.* 1630-35) Zurbarán painted *Christ on the Cross* for the Capuchin monastery in Seville. It is one of the five canvases belonging to the Museum which he may have painted with the assistance of members of his workshop. In these highly *tenebrist* works the figure of Christ crucified – with four nails, as prescribed by Pacheco – stands out against a dark background with almost sculptural intensity.

Zurbarán continued to work for the Dominicans and in 1636 produced *The Blessed*

Francisco de Zurbarán. *Christ on the Cross* (c. 1630-35).

Zurbarán's workshop.
St Dorothy (*c.* 1650).

throne of golden clouds surrounded by the customary cherubim. Another painting – *Christ Crowning St Joseph* – has also been associated with this altarpiece. A work displaying extremely delicate colours, it demonstrates Zurbarán's great skill in depicting the faces and hands of his figures.

From a slightly later date is *Our Lady of the Rosary* (*c.* 1645-50), one of Zurbarán's finest interpretations of the Virgin and Child theme. As was often the case in his work, the delicate composition is based on an engraving, enhanced through the more fluent technique and harmony of colour typical of his mature years.

Another series of three canvases which, due to their technical and compositional characteristics, were originally believed to date from his early period, are in fact from around 1655. Painted for the Charterhouse of Santa María de las Cuevas in Seville, *St Bruno's Visit to Urban II*, *Our Lady of the Carthusians* and *St Hugo in the Refectory* reveal Zurbarán's masterly interpretation of the spiritual principles governing the lives of the Carthusians: silence, devotion to the Virgin Mary and mortification of the flesh through fasting. Their inherent simplicity and imperfections are more than made up for by the painter's extraordinary mastery of the qualities of the paint and his power to convey each element as unique and individual. The light, flowing technique reveals a distancing from his initial *tenebrism* and contrasts of light and shade, the result being light-filled compositions displaying carefully chosen colours.

They were many followers of the style which earned Zurbarán his reputation, the best-known being his son Juan de Zurbarán, Francisco Reyna, the Polanco brothers (Francisco and Miguel), Bernabé de Ayala and

Enrique Susón and *St Luis Bertran* for the transept altars of the Portacoelli monastery church. Here the figures, which he painted after his enlightening visit to the royal collections at Court in Madrid, appear against a light-filled landscape with scenes alluding to episodes in their lives.

Soon after this (*c.* 1640) Zurbarán painted his monumental *Eternal Father* for the upper section of the altarpiece of the church of another Seville monastery, the San José de Mercedarios Descalzos. Here the majestic figure sits on a

FRANCISCO DE ZURBARÁN. ST HUGO IN THE REFECTORY (c. 1655).

Ignacio de Ríes. By one of these or perhaps by members of Zurbarán's workshop with some degree of participation by the master himself, is a series of saints now belonging to the Museum. As the figures in the paintings suggest a procession, in all likelihood they were intended for the nave of a church. Also inspired by Zurbarán's style is a picture of the *Apostles* attributed to Francisco Polanco (Cazorla, Jaén, c. 1610-Seville 1651).

– High Baroque

In Seville, development towards the dynamic and spectacular forms of Baroque was furthered in 1654 by Herrera the Younger and the work of its two main exponents: Murillo and Valdés Leal. Murillo's style was to predominate during the second half of the century, his very pure technique applied to the cultivation of a gentle, delicate form of art which became highly popular in a city devastated by hardship and suffering. Valdés's expressiveness and vigorous, passionate style was also warmly received.

Francisco de Herrera the Younger (Seville 1627-Madrid 1685). (Room VI)

The son of Herrera the Elder, Francisco Herrera the Younger received his training at his father's workshop and in Italy, although he ultimately settled in Madrid in 1650. He belonged to the first generation of artists who brought a process of renewal to painting in Madrid through the introduction of a new, fully Baroque idiom.

His dynamic, somewhat affected compositions, multiple back lighting effects and fluent strokes of vibrant colour were greatly admired in Seville when he returned to the city in 1654. The "fiery" style of *The Triumph of the Eucharist* (1656) and *St Francis in Glory* (1657), which he painted for the Cathedral, initiated a new path in painting which was soon followed by Murillo and Valdés. In all likelihood he painted *St Thomas Aquinas* when still in Seville. He remained there until 1660, when he is mentioned as one of the founders of the new Academy of Painting, although this was also the year of his definitive return to Madrid.

Bartolomé Esteban Murillo (Seville 1617-1682). (Rooms V and VII)

Without any doubt Murillo is one of the most important figures in Spanish painting and the Museum's major collection of his work one of its greatest attractions.

Born in Seville late in 1617, Murillo received his training at Juan del Castillo's workshop. His early style followed that of Zurbarán with paintings full of rigorous *tenebrist* naturalism and the coloured clouds suffused with golden light often found in the work of Roelas. The Museum possesses a number of his early works, including a *Virgin of the Immaculate Conception* also known as "The Colossal" (*c.* 1650) from the Monastery of San Francisco in Seville. Although Murillo based this theme on the model created by Ribera, he established a new iconographic prototype with paintings full of dynamism characterized by flowing white robes and blue mantles and angels hovering around the Virgin Mary.

Another example of his little-known early production is *The Ecstasy of St Francis* (*c.* 1645-1650), acquired by the Spanish state in 1994. Originally belonging to Diego Maestre, a Sevillian collector and contemporary of the painter's, it is a further example of Ribera's influence as seen, according to Angulo, in the technical treatment of the work and in the saint's face.

The large number of major commissions Murillo received in the course of his career testify to the city's great prestige. The Museum possesses the high altarpiece paintings from the series he was commissioned to paint for the church of the Monastery of San Agustín in Seville in 1664. *St Augustine and the Trinity* depicts the vision which inspired the saint to write his treatise "De Trinitate", while in *St Augustine with the Virgin and Child* Augustine is shown offering the Virgin his heart, which is pierced by a dart of love, as a token of devotion to her. For a chapel in the same church he also painted the St Thomas of Villanueva altarpiece,

(Opposite) Francisco de Herrera the Younger. *St Thomas Aquinas* (*c.* 1656).

Bartolomé Esteban Murillo.
St Thomas of Villanueva Giving Alms (1668-69).

from which the Museum possesses one of the two predella paintings, *St Thomas of Villanueva and the Crucifix* (*c.* 1665-70).

The Museum's most important group of paintings by Murillo came from the altars in the sacristy and side chapels of the Capuchin monastery church in Seville. Painted between 1665 and 1669, when Murillo was in his artistic prime, they are among the best of his entire production.

These paintings were saved from the French during the invasion of Spain and subsequently restored by the Sevillian painter Joaquín Bejarano, to whom the friars showed their appreci-

ation with a gift of the central painting from the high altarpiece, *The Jubilee of the Portiuncula*, which is now in the Wallraff-Richard Museum, Cologne. In the Museum this painting has been substituted by "The Colossal" *Virgin of the Immaculate Conception* painted by Murillo for the local Monastery of San Francisco around 1650. The lower section of the high altarpiece contained the *Holy Face* with *Our Lady of the Napkin* above it, and *S.S. Justa and Rufina* (popular Sevillian prototypes of beauty) to its left and *S.S. Leander and Bonaventura* (patron saints of the city) to the right. In the second section were *St Joseph and the Child* on the right and *St John the Baptist* on the left, with *St Anthony and the Child* and *St Felix of Cantalicio and the Child* above these in lunettes subsequently adapted into rectangles.

For the presbytery altarpieces Murillo painted an *Annunciation*, a *Pietà*, *St Michael the Archangel* and *The Guardian Angel*, while the side chapel altars displayed other paintings of his. The north chapels contained *St Anthony and the Child*, *The Virgin Mary of the Eternal Father* and *St Francis Embracing the Crucified Christ*, while the south chapels contained *The Adoration of the Shepherds*, *St Felix of Cantalicio Embracing the Child*, and, next to the main entrance, an excellent painting of *St Thomas of Villanueva*, Murillo's favourite canvas and a brilliant synthesis of all his work. The *Virgin of the Immaculate Conception*, the last painting in this excellent series painted for the Capuchins, was situated in the choir.

The magnificent depictions of the saints in this series and the complex interplay of light in some of the scenes – as in the *Nativity* and *St Thomas of Villanueva* – are clearly the result of Murillo's artistic maturity, a technical maturity

(Opposite) Bartolomé Esteban Murillo.
"The Colossal" Virgin of the Immaculate Conception (*c.* 1650).

Bartolomé Esteban Murillo. *Virgin and Child* ("*Our Lady of the Napkin*") (1665-66).

revealed, furthermore, in the exceptional fluency of the "vaporous" brush-strokes with which he dissolved forms and anticipated the sensitivities of the coming century.

Other fine examples of Murillo's work are a *Mater Dolorosa* (*c.* 1665) donated to the Museum, in which the figure of the Virgin, particu-larly her face and hands, is illuminated against a dark background (yet again revealing Murillo's mastery of *chiaroscuro*), and *St Jerome* (*c.* 1665), which was acquired by the Spanish state in 1972. The Museum also possesses a number of paintings from his workshop and by anonymous followers.

Bartolomé Esteban Murillo. *S.S. Justa and Rufina* (1665-66).

Disciples and Followers of Murillo
(Rooms VI and VII)

From the middle of the 17th century, Sevillian artists gradually began to abandon Zurbarán's style to follow in Murillo's footsteps. The huge success of Murillo's models and methods, based on a pleasing and simple idiom which touched the sentiments of the faithful in accordance with the principles of the Counter-Reformation, had a profound effect on Seville's art circles, and his influence was to continue well into the 18th and even the 19th centuries. Nevertheless, the work of his followers was generally confined to imitations of his compositions and models rather than of his style as a whole.

Cornelius Schut (Antwerp 1629-Seville 1685) was one of the most important representatives of this circle, although due to his extremely faithful imitation of Murillo's style, a number of his works were once attributed to the master himself. Of these the Museum possesses a portrait of *Friar Dominic of Brussels*, signed and dated by Schut in 1665, a *Virgin of the Immaculate Conception* (*c.* 1680) and a *Sleeping Christ Child* (*c.* 1675) that is extremely reminiscent of his style.

Although primarily a follower of Murillo, Matías de Arteaga (Villanueva de los Infantes, Ciudad Real 1633-Seville 1703) also assimilated some of the expressive features of Valdés Leal's style. In 1869 the Museum acquired six of his twelve paintings of the *Life of the Virgin* (*c.* 1680) from the Church of San Marcos in Seville. These display elements typical of his production, with broad architectural perspectives, chequered floors and small figures similar to Valdés Leal's.

Pedro Núñez de Villavicencio (Seville 1640-*c.* 1695) is the best-known of Murillo's disciples. His style, however, is a mixture of the influence of Murillo and the Italian Mattia Preti, whom he met on a visit to Italy. Murillo's influence is particularly noteworthy in his genre or street scenes, as in the Museum's *The Wine-seller* (*c.* 1685). One example of Italian influence in his work is *Judith with the Head of Holofernes* (1674), a painting full of drama and *chiaroscuro*.

One faithful follower of Murillo's active at the turn of the 17th century was Francisco Meneses Osorio (Seville 1640-1721). The Museum possesses a number of his works,

including *St Joseph and the Child* (1684), the *Infant St John the Baptist* (*c.* 1685), *The Appearance of Our Lady of Mercy to St Peter Nolasco* (*c.* 1690) and *St Cyril of Alexandria at the Council of Ephesus* (1701).

The Museum also possesses a number of fine paintings by Juan Simón Gutiérrez (Medina Sidonia, Cadiz, 1643-Seville 1718), among these *S.S. Joaquim and Anne* (*c.* 1700) and a monumental *St Dominic Comforted by the Virgin and Female Martyred Saints* (1710).

The large number of paintings by Esteban Márquez (Puebla de Guzmán, Huelva 1652-Seville 1696) which belong to the Museum suggests that he ran a very busy workshop in Seville. Although the figures in his paintings reflect Murillo's influence, they are characterized and differentiated by certain typical physical features and a gentle form of expressiveness.

The examples of his work date from his later period and include *St Augustine and the Mystery of the Trinity* (*c.* 1690) and *The Appearance of Christ and the Virgin to St Augustine* (*c.* 1690), both from the Monastery of San Agustín in Seville. Also exhibited is *St Joseph and the Child* (*c.* 1690) from the Monastery of San Antonio Abad.

By Sebastián Gómez (Granada *c.* 1665-Seville *c.* 1720), whose byname was "the Mulatto", the Museum possesses a signed large-format and somewhat affected canvas of *Our Lady of the Rosary and St Dominic* (1690) originally from the Monastery of San Pablo in Seville. Furthermore, the style of a *Virgin of the Immaculate Conception* (*c.* 1700), from the Capuchin monastery also in Seville, is very similar to Gómez's.

Francisco Antolínez (Seville *c.* 1644-Madrid *c.* 1700) specialized in series of Gospel and

(Opposite) Pedro Núñez de Villavicencio. *The Wine-seller* (*c.* 1685).

Juan de Valdés Leal. *The Temptations of St Jerome* (1657).

Old Testament scenes usually in the form of decorative, small-format paintings with special emphasis on the religious theme as opposed to the landscape, *Jacob with Laban's Flock* being one clear example. This type of painting with small figures against architectural backgrounds or blurred landscapes made Antolínez a major exponent of the dynamic style typical of the Sevillian school of the turn of the 17th century.

From a previous generation and therefore uninfluenced by Murillo, Pedro Camprobín Passano (Almagro, Ciudad Real 1605-Seville 1674) was an exponent of a genre which reached its height in the 17th century – the *bodegón*. Exquisite sensitivity and intimist refinement characterize the complex, flower-filled compositions with landscapes and architectural settings typical of his mature years. One fine example is exhibited in the Museum.

JUAN DE VALDÉS LEAL. *THE FLAGELLATION OF ST JEROME* (1657).

Juan de Valdés Leal (Seville 1622-1690)
(Room VIII)

Juan de Valdés Leal was born in Seville in 1622 and died there in 1690. In 1647 he travelled to Córdoba, where he developed a style reflecting the influence of both the dominant naturalism of the Sevillian school and that of the most prominent painter in the Córdoba of the times, Antonio del Castillo. His first known works include major series for the Convent of Santa Clara in Carmona (1652-53) and the altarpiece of the Convent of El Carmen in Córdoba (1655-58).

He settled in Seville in 1657, becoming so involved with the city's art circles that by 1660 he had founded the Academy of Painting with Murillo and Herrera the Younger (and later became its director). Valdés reached his artistic prime in the 1660s, a decade in which he recei-

JUAN DE VALDÉS LEAL.
THE ASSUMPTION OF THE VIRGIN (1670-72).

ved important commissions for individual paintings and series. With disentailment, a number of these pictures came into the Museum's possession. They include a very interesting cycle of scenes from the life of St Jerome from the sacristy of the Monastery of San Jerónimo de Buenavista in Seville (1657) and another of St Ignatius (1660-1664) from the Jesuit Casa Profesa, also in Seville.

Consisting of eighteen canvases on episodes from the saint's life, the former extols the history of the religious order through depictions of its principal members, some directly associated with the monastery itself. Half of the series was acquired by the Museum in the wake of the Disentailment Act in 1840 while the other was sold illegally to collectors.

The series begins with *The Baptism of St Jerome*, signed and dated by Valdés in 1657. Of higher quality are the scenes of the *Temptation* and the *Flagellation*, which display the dramatic intensity and vigorous colour characteristic of his work. Outside Spain are *St Jerome Disputing with the Rabbis* and *The Death of St Jerome*.

The Museum's paintings of prominent members of the Order include the portraits of the first prior, Fray Pedro Fernández Pecha, the second prior and founder of the Monastery of Guadalupe, Fray Fernando Yáñez de Figueroa, Fray Hernando de Talavera, Bishop of Granada, Fray Alonso Fernández Pecha, and Fray Juan de Ledesma, who is depicted grappling with a snake which had terrorized local villagers.

The *Life of San Ignatius Loyola* series (1660-64), which Valdés painted for the courtyard of the Jesuit Casa Profesa in Seville, is surpassed by his series on St Jerome, due to the fact that he received small remuneration for it and that long years of exposure to the elements and a number of ill-advised restoration projects have led to its sorry state of conservation. Nevertheless, Valdés's mastery is still evident in some fragments of the better paintings from the series, particularly *St Ignatius Doing Penance in the Cave at Manresa* and *The Appearance of Christ to St Ignatius on the Way to Rome*.

Between 1674 and 1676 Valdés painted two more pictures for the Casa Profesa: *S.S. Ignatius and Francis Borgia Contemplating an Allegory of the Eucharist* and *St Ignatius Contemplating the Monogram of Christ*.

JUAN DE VALDÉS LEAL. *Our Lady with St John and the Two Marys on the Way to Calvary* (c. 1659).

The Immaculate Conception and *The Assumption of the Virgin* (1670-72) for the side altarpieces of the Monastery of San Agustín in Seville are possibly Valdés's best altar paintings. In these dynamic although somewhat affected compositions the effects of light and shade are particularly striking with respect to the figures set against backgrounds of flowing, form-dissolving brush-strokes.

In 1673 Valdés painted seven pictures of the life of St Ambrose for the *Bishop Ambrosio de Spínola Altarpiece* in the lower oratory of the Archbishop's Palace in Seville. Acquired by the Museum in 1991, the first, entitled *The Miracle of the Bees*, reveals the sketching tech-

nique and enormous expressiveness of Valdés's style.

The Museum also possesses a collection of exceptional individual works which include the deeply dramatic *Our Lady with St John and the Two Marys on the Way to Calvary* (c. 1659), *St Francis Receiving the Water Bottle* (c. 1665) and *The Mystic Marriage of St Catherine* (c. 1685). Of the few examples of portraits painted by Valdés the Museum possesses *Fray Alonso de Sotomayor y Caro* (1657). As the friar is depicted in the upper choir of the Monastery of La Merced Calzada church, the painting offers a glimpse of how the area, which is now the main room in the Museum, was decorated in the 17th century.

Francisco Barrera. *Spring* (1638).

Finally, among the donation of Valdés's work made to the Museum, *The Workshop in Nazareth* (1680-85), which was apparently based on an original engraving by Ribera, displays expressive figures characteristic of Valdés's style.

In 1672 Valdés received a commission for the Church of La Caridad, which his friend Miguel de Mañara had recently converted into a hospital. Mañara was the author of *Discourse of Truth*, a treatise that was to inspire Valdés's "Hieroglyphs of Death and Salvation", two canvases in which he portrayed death with chilling realism.

These two works reveal Valdés's artistic personality, his direct vigorous style, fluent economical technique, and the rich colour of his dynamic compositions – thanks to which he is known as one of Spanish Baroque painting's prime representatives.

The Madrid School

The other great 17th-century group of artists represented in the Museum is that of the Madrid school. One of its major exponents was José Antolínez (Madrid 1635-1675), who painted an elegant *Mary Magdalene* (1673) and a *Virgin of the Immaculate Conception* (*c.* 1670), a theme on which he produced numerous, highly personal variations. Two paintings by another member, Francisco Gutiérrez, famous for his highly imaginative architectural structures, are also exhibited in the Museum. The

FRANCISCO BARRERA. *SUMMER* (1638).

first depicts the triumphal entrance of *Joseph in Heliopolis* (1657), inspired by the passage from Genesis, while the second, *The Fall of Troy* (1657), represents the famous scene from Virgil's *Aeneid*.

A highly successful genre in the 17th century, the *bodegón* (scenes of daily life with strong elements of still life in the composition) is represented by *The Four Seasons* series (1638), painted by another Madrid artist, Francisco Barrera, who lived and worked in Seville between 1635 and 1645.

Another major centre of painting in Spain was Toledo, birthplace of Luis Tristán (*c.* 1585-1634), who studied at El Greco's workshop. The Museum possesses a beautiful *Virgin of the Immaculate Conception* by him.

José de Ribera (Játiva, Valencia 1591-Naples 1652)

It was in Valencia, another great centre of art, where José Ribera embarked on his career, although he was to spend most of his life in Naples in the service of the Viceroys of Spain. Italian influence was crucial to the formation of his style and sensitivities, but he nevertheless signed all his paintings with his Spanish name. Those works of his which were shipped to Spain had considerable influence on other artists there. His early paintings prove him to be a follower of Caravaggio, whose *tenebrist* form of naturalism is evident in Ribera's work, as is a certain Roman-Bolognian classicism and Venetian pictorialism and colour.

PIETER VAN LINT. *ADORATION OF THE SHEPHERDS* (*c.* 1650).

There are numerous instances of individual figures of saints in his paintings, one being the Museum's serene, well-balanced portrait of *St James the Apostle* (*c.* 1634). Quite startling in this painting is Ribera's skilful use of light and the powerful modelling of his confident lines – for which his mastery as an engraver must also have been essential. The sobriety of the composition draws the attention to the basic elements of the picture while the densely-applied brush-strokes recreate the qualities of the material.

A further example of his work is *St Teresa of Jesus*, which he signed and dated in 1630, while a *St Sebastian* is highly suggestive of his style and may therefore be attributable to him.

- ROOM IX.
  EUROPEAN BAROQUE PAINTING

The Museum's European Baroque works form an interesting collection of mainly Flemish and Italian paintings representative of the art produced beyond Spain's frontiers during the 16th and 17th centuries.

The Flemish School

The 17th-century Flemish school is represented by the Antwerp-born Pieter van Lint's (1609-1690) *Adoration of the Shepherds* (*c.* 1650). The influence of the school's great master, Rubens, on his style is evident in this painting, as is that

José de Ribera. *St James the Apostle* (c. 1634).

Jan Bruegel the Elder.
The Earthly Paradise (*c.* 1620).

of the Italian masters – due to Lint's long stay in Italy. Rubens's influence is again evident in the *Adoration of the Magi* (*c.* 1645) by Cornelis de Vos (1585-1651), another painter who worked in collaboration with the master. After Rubens's death, de Vos specialized in portraits, *The Lady*, exhibited in this room, being one fine example.

Landscape painting is represented by *A Village Garden*, in a style similar to that of Jan Wildens (1568-1653), and also by the excellent *Adam and Eve in Paradise* (*c.* 1610) and *Landscape with Animals* (*c.* 1620) both painted by Jan Bruegel the Elder (1568-1625), an artist who specialized in religious, allegorical and mythological scenes with small landscape backgrounds. Landscape also served as a background to the battle scenes for which Sebastian Vranckx (1573-1647) created a prototype.

Cornelis Norbertus Gysbrechts (1610-1675) specialized in another very popular Baroque theme, the *bodegón*. By him the Museum possesses an interesting *Vanitas* – a theme typical of the moralizing tendency of European Baroque.

The Italian School

The Italian school best represented in the Museum is that of Naples, one of whose members was Giovanni Battista Caracciolo (Naples 1578-1637). His *Head of John the Baptist* (*c.* 1630) proves him a follower of Caravaggio's form of *tenebrist* naturalism. The same manner of depicting figures and objects against dark backgrounds and accentuating them with direct, often dazzling light was also used by Matta Preti (Taverna, Calabria 1613-Valleta 1699) in his *Christ Risen in the Cenacle* (*c.* 1675).

As *Tenebrism* ignored landscape and instead highlighted objects, the still life as a genre reached a high degree of development in Baroque art. One interesting example is *Still Life with Grapes and Apples* (*c.* 1670), attributed to Gian Battista Ruoppolo (Naples 1628-1693). Another is two highly refined paintings by Margarita Caffi (Milan 1651-1710) both entitled *Flower Vase*.

Classicism, the other main tendency in Italian painting, is represented by Andrea Vaccaro's (Naples 1604-1670) *Jonah Preaching to the People of Nineveh* (*c.* 1645).

- Room X
  Baroque Sculpture

The sculpture produced in 17th-century Spain was almost exclusively religious. Art was

Giovanni Battista Caracciolo. *The Head of John the Baptist* (1638).

placed at the service of the Counter-Reformation, whose aim was to influence the faithful through the realism of the religious scene depicted. Baroque interest in life and nature led also to that same desire for realism and a sensation of movement, and to pictorial effects which found one of their highest forms of expression in carved and painted wood.

Once carved, sculptures of this kind were painted by accomplished artists who sought the effects of light and shade most capable of endowing them with the highest possible degree of naturalism. This exaltation of realism frequently led to the addition of artificial elements

like hair, eyes and tears and ultimately to the "clothed image" so popular in the 17th and 18th centuries. During this period of religious exaltation, some figures, whether individually or in groups, served as focal points for demonstrations of faith in the streets.

The generation of Mannerist masters active in the last third of the 16th century, during the reign of Philip II, was followed by another whose work, with classicistic principles as their starting point, developed towards forms endowed with greater vitality and expressiveness. Furthermore, the models of late-Mannerism were gradually abandoned in the 17th-century and altarpieces were transformed into the monumental architectural pieces typical of high Baroque.

The Sevillian School

The generation of Sevillian early-Baroque sculptors was led by Gaspar Núñez Delgado, Andrés Ocampo and Juan de Oviedo the Younger, whose work reveals a preoccupation with the naturalism which was finally to become predominant thanks to the school's most outstanding figure, Juan Martínez Montañés.

Juan Martínez Montañés (Alcalá la Real, Jaén 1564-Seville 1649) received his early training at Pablo de Rojas's workshop in Granada and came to Seville when still very young, obtaining his master sculptor's certificate at the age of nineteen. As an artist he was highly respected by his contemporaries, who dubbed him "the god of wood carving" and "the Andalusian Lysippus". In Seville he was influenced by the generation of late-Mannerist sculptors, while his knowledge of 16th-century sculpture is evident in the serenity and severe classicism which characterize his work.

His first Mannerist sculptures, which include a *St. Christopher* (1597) from the Church of El Salvador in Seville, were followed by veritable masterpieces characterized by their elegance and sober sense of balance.

A commission in 1603 for his magnificent *Crucified Christ of Clemency* was followed a few years later by another for his extremely delicate *Christ Child Giving His Blessing* (1606-1607) for the local "Brotherhood of the Sacrarium". Both served as iconographic models for the subsequent generations of sculptors. His most famous processional sculptures are the *Christ of Passion*

and the extremely beautiful *"La Cieguecita" Virgin Mary* (1628), carved for Seville Cathedral.

As a maker of altarpieces Montañés set a new trend in these Italian-inspired structures, adapting them to his own personal idiom. His most outstanding works of this kind are the high altarpieces for the Sevillian Monastery of San Isidore del Campo (1609) and the Church of San Miguel, Jerez (1641).

The Museum possesses a number of exceptional pieces by Montañés. After the Disentailment Act of 1835, *St Dominic Flagellating Himself* (*c.* 1606-1607), which was coloured by Pacheco, came to the Museum from the high altarpiece of the local Monastery of Portacoeli. Here echoes of the iconographic models of Torrigiani's *St Jerome* are present in the kneeling figure of the saint, who holds a crucifix in his left hand and a scourge for flagellating his back in his right. The highly expressive head is a fine example of the restrained naturalism common in Montañés's masterpieces of that time; a perfectly accomplished naturalism also applied to the modelling of the saint's torso, in contrast with the sobriety and the effects of light and shade in the folds of the habit.

In 1634 Montañés carved a statue of the Carthusian Order's founder, *St Bruno*, for the Charterhouse of Santa María de las Cuevas. All the naturalist power in it is concentrated in the magnificent head of the saint, who stands with a crucifix in his right hand and the ordinance of the Order in his left.

Expressive realism, elegance and balanced volumes come together in this, a piece which reveals the development of Montañés's work towards Baroque realism in the final years of his long career.

Juan Martínez Montañés. *St Bruno* (1634).

In 1972 the Museum acquired the *St John the Baptist Altarpiece* (1610-1620) from the local Convent of Santa María del Socorro. Montañés was commissioned to carve it in 1610, while Juan de Uceda's task was to paint the thirteen small panels illustrating different scenes from the saint's life. Based architecturally on the Italian late-Renaissance altarpiece-portal, it is very similar to the one Montañés carved for Lima cathedral in Peru years later.

The nine scenes from the saint's life reflect Montañés's customary use of low relief for the secondary scenes and high relief and *ronde-bosse* for the figures in the central niches. The main *Baptism* scene – the forerunner of the one on the high altarpiece in Santiponce – is particularly beautiful.

An outstanding disciple of Montañés's was Juan de Mesa (Córdoba 1583-Seville 1627), who with the serene, classicistic models of his master as his starting point, introduced the Sevillian school to the highly expressive power of naturalism. His method of taking elements from life to express the spiritual experience made him the perfect interpreter of the Counter-Reformation's aims. Such characteristics are especially evident in the large number of crucified Christs he carved for the Sevillian penitent brotherhoods. Especially outstanding among this rich group of images are the *"Christ of Love"* from the parish Church of El Salvador, the *"Christ of the Good Death"*, which now belongs to Seville University, the *"Christ of the Conversion of the Penitent Thief"* from the Church of Montserrat, *"Christ of Vergara"* and the unforgettable *"Jesus of Great Power"*.

Two of the images by Mesa in the Museum reveal the influence of Montañés. Originally from the two altarpieces of the lay brothers' choir of the Charterhouse of Santa María de las Cuevas, they are *Our Lady of Las Cuevas* and *St John the Baptist*. Although Montañés was originally chosen to carve them, for some reason he was unable to do so and Mesa signed a new contract with the Charterhouse to make them in 1623. Through the images he paid tribute to the serenity of his master's figures through forms with balanced volumes and a simple naturalist idiom full of contained expressiveness.

His own artistic personality is evident, however, in the diagonal composition of the Virgin Mary and the expressive energy of the Baptist's head, whose intense gaze and tousled hair accentuate the work's Baroque character.

Another magnificent work by Mesa is his image of *St Raymund Nonnatus*, commissioned by the Mercedarian Church of San José, Seville, in 1626. In accordance with the terms of the contract, Mesa modelled the saint in a Mercedarian habit, a mozzetta and a cardinal's hat, with a book in his left hand and a monstrance in his right.

The lips must originally have been secured with a padlock – one of the saint's attributes as he was tortured in this way as punishment for preaching. Quite startling in this work which reveals the mastery of Mesa's mature years is the powerful head and the dynamic modelling of the mozzetta and Mercedarian habit.

Dating from around 1627 are three clothed images from the Casa Profesa of the Jesuit saints *St Paul Miki*, *St John Soan Goto* and *St James Kisai* which reached the Museum through the González Abreu legacy. Although once attributed jointly to Montañés and Mesa, it is now thought that Mesa either made all three or alternatively the first two and Montañés the third.

JUAN DE MESA. *ST RAYMUND NONNATUS* (1626).

Juan de Solís (Jaén 1580?-Seville 1621?) was one of the many young sculptors from Montañés's workshop who assimilated the master's aesthetics and technique. Commissioned with Montañés and Mesa to make a number of pieces for the Charterhouse of Santa María de las Cuevas, in 1616 he carved the *Cardinal Virtues* above the two altarpieces of the lay brothers' choir. Particularly interesting due to their meticulousness and expressive power are the recumbent allegorical figures on consoles similar to those devised by Michelangelo.

Emphasis on realism, movement and drama in the Spanish sculpture of the mid-17th century marks the formal change to high Baroque. It was José de Arce, a Flemish sculptor trained in Rome, who introduced the new forms to Seville through the altarpiece for the Church of San Miguel in Jerez which Montañés had been unable to complete.

This new idiom became consolidated with Pedro Roldán (Seville 1624-1699), a Seville-born sculptor who trained in Alonso de Mena's workshop in Granada. His large-scale compositions, like the *Pietà* originally in the Chapel of Los Vizcaínos and now in the Cathedral sanctuary, or the altarpiece of the local Hospital de La Caridad confirmed the new style.

Dynamism, extraordinary naturalism and extremely lifelike attitudes characterize these groups of figures whose most innovative feature was the sense of drama they conveyed.

The Museum possesses a *Bust of a Saint* attributed by Hernández Díaz to Roldán. A highly expressive work, it appears to have a great deal in common with the group of figures on the high altarpiece in the Hospital de la Caridad.

Two followers of Roldán – Antonio Ruiz Gijón (Utrera, Seville 1653-*c.* 1720) and Pedro Duque Cornejo (Seville 1678-1757) – bring this look at Sevillian Baroque sculpture to an end. The expressive, dynamic works of the latter, who was Roldán's grandson, ensured the existence of Sevillian Baroque until well after the beginning of 18th century.

The Granada School

An important member of this new school was Alonso de Mena (Granada 1587-1646), and it was in Mena's workshop where his son Pedro, Bernardo de Mora and Pedro Roldán all received their training.

However, its most prominent member was to be Alonso Cano (Granada 1601-1667), whose arrival in Granada in 1652 brought far-reaching changes to the school. In spite of their highly personal styles, the pupils confined themselves to following and reinterpreting the master's methods. Of this group, the artist most closely associated with Cano was Pedro de Mena (Granada 1628-Malaga 1688), who also worked in collaboration with him on a number of projects.

Mena's life and work as a sculptor were closely linked to two cities – Granada and Malaga – and it was in the latter where he carved one of his most outstanding works, the Cathedral's choir stalls. Although on occasions he emulated the sculptures of others, he also produced works of his own, proving himself an artist in his own right. Among his more personal and most frequently repeated creations are the *Mater Dolorosa* and *Ecce Homo* panels, generally of bust- and life-size figures often placed together. Works such as these led to the prevalence of the devotional image, made especially for the faithful to approach and contemplate.

PEDRO DE MENA. *MATER DOLOROSA* (*c.* 1658-70).

Thanks to the González-Abreu donation the Museum possesses one such *Mater Dolorosa* (*c.* 1658-70) which, although undocumented, is attributed to Mena. In this half-bust version the hands are crossed at the centre and the figure faces the front, while the colours are the customary ones used in this type of figure – vivid crimson for the robe, white for the head-dress and blue for the mantle. These elements frame the face and focus the attention on the Virgin's expression of pent-up grief and pain.

Also from the González-Abreu collection is an *Infant St John the Baptist* signed and dated by Mena in Malaga in 1674.

Despite the typically Andalusian devotion to images of children, Mena rarely dealt with this theme. Here the clothed figure displays the features characteristic of Mena's style: bulging forehead, almond eyes, small mouth with thin lips, a cross in the left hand and a right hand – in this case missing – pointing to a lamb at the saint's feet.

18TH-CENTURY PAINTING

• Room XI •

The Sevillian School

Francisco de Goya y Lucientes

• ROOM XI

For Spain the new century brought a change in the reigning dynasty with the Bourbons succeeding the Spanish Habsburgs. This prompted an influx of foreign artists mainly from France and Italy who, to the detriment of their Spanish counterparts, were the beneficiaries of all the commissions awarded and the only artists to prosper in the new circumstances. Goya was the only Spanish painter with sufficient personality to rebel against this situation.

The invasion of foreign artists came as a turning-point for the arts in Spain and had far-reaching effects on the field of painting. At Court the kind of painter most in demand was the portraitist and in this respect Velázquez had unfortunately left no successors. The portraiture of

LUCAS VALDÉS.
ST ELIZABETH OF HUNGARY HEALING A SICK PERSON (c. 1720).

this period became more of an instrument to glorify the 18th-century monarchy than to capture the sitter's actual likeness and so proved incompatible with the traditional approach of the painters of the Spanish school.

Thus, with the monopoly first of the French and subsequently of the Italians, the purer forms of Spanish art began to fade.

The Sevillian School

It has long been said that with the death of Murillo the Sevillian school disappeared and even that it did not make a comeback until the early 19th century. Seville, however, resisted foreign influence by remaining faithful to its traditions and even became the main purveyor of Spanish national art.

Eighteenth-century Sevillian painting can be divided into two different periods, the first dominated by the tradition of Murillo and Valdés Leal and the second by Rococo and Neo-Classical art. Murillo's work, nevertheless, continued to be copied until well after the beginning of the 19th century.

Not surprisingly, Murillo's influence continued to exert itself on Sevillian painters during the first half of the century, as most of the master's disciples and followers reached their prime during this time.

Due apparently to Seville's economic situation, the work of these painters was confined to routine copying devoid of all creativity and incapable of surpassing the work of the master. Thus the art of those years saw little renovation and was of a low standard.

It was to this background that Lucas Valdés (Seville 1661-Cadiz 1725), the son of Juan de

LUCAS VALDÉS. *ALLEGORY OF THE INSTITUTION OF THE THIRD ORDER* (c. 1720).

Valdés Leal, lived and worked. Valdés is one of the most typical representatives of the first period mentioned above, for although among the few artists not influenced by Murillo, he was nevertheless a follower of his father's techniques. In mural painting, his main field of activity, he earned himself a well-deserved reputation and received commissions for some of Seville's most important buildings and monuments.

By Valdés the Museum possesses a cycle of twelve paintings of scenes from the *Life of St Francis of Paola* originally from the Minim monastery in Seville. Although some are rather careless in execution, they are of considerable interest where iconography is concerned, as the miracle scenes are illustrated in great detail.

The Museum's most typical paintings of Lucas Valdés's style are *Allegory of the Institution of the Third Order* and *St Elizabeth of Hungary Healing a Sick Person*, both highly ambitious compositions with interesting iconography. The setting and date for the former must have been the Portiuncula in 1221; in it a seated St Francis is shown giving the rule to one of the first members of the Third Order – either Matteo de Rubeis, who kneels before him, or the blessed Luquesio de Poggi-Bonci. A number of male and female saints of the Third Franciscan Order witness the event, among them St Elizabeth of Hungary and St Louis, King of France, both of whom are venerated as special patrons of the Order.

Domingo Martínez. *Carriage of the Homage of Apollo and the Three Noble Arts to the New Monarchs* (c. 1748).

The setting for the second painting is the gallery of a courtyard with a double arcade, possibly in the hospital founded by the saint in Marburg, Germany. The central scene shows St Elizabeth with her maids amid a group of the sick and poor as they wash and attend to a patient. Before them is a basket containing bread, the symbol of charity. To the left, a scene in the background illustrates one of the saint's miracles as recounted by Dietrich d'Apolda: the transformation in the presence of Elizabeth's husband, King Louis IV of Thuringia, of a leper she had lain in their own bed, into the figure of the Crucified Christ. Due to their iconography both paintings may have been originally intended for a chapel of the Tertiary Order in one of the Franciscan monasteries in Seville. They reached the Museum in 1840 in the wake of the 1836 disentailment of church possessions.

Although born in Cadiz, Clemente Torres (Cadiz 1662?-1730) received his training in Seville at Juan de Valdés Leal's workshop, where he was a friend and fellow-disciple of Lucas Valdés's. He and Valdés the Younger are considered the best fresco painters of their generation. The Museum possesses two paintings attributed to Torres: *St Nicholas of Bari* and *St Dionysius the Areopagite*. The former depicts a vigorous, dynamic style full of fluent, very colourful strokes, clearly influenced by the master. The latter, however, has little in common with it and is highly stylized, cold and almost lifeless.

A minor painter, Andrés Pérez (Seville 1660-1727) received his Murillo-influenced training in Seville. He developed a style very much his own and far-removed from the master's, although the lines of his figures do display a certain amiable expressiveness. The iconography of the Museum's best paintings by Pérez – *Abraham before Melchizedek* and *David before Ahimelech* (c. 1720) – is interesting as both paintings have a distinctly "eucharistic" air about them and display spacious architectural backgrounds executed with a fine sense of perspective. The first illustrates Genesis 14: 17-20 in which Abraham, having defeated the Elamites, comes forward to

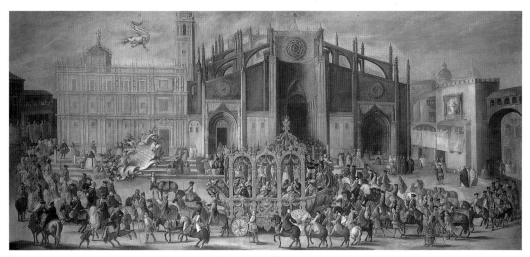

DOMINGO MARTÍNEZ. *Carriage of the Herald of the Masque* (c. 1748).

DOMINGO MARTÍNEZ. *Carriage of the Delivery of the Portraits of the King and Queen to the Town Hall* (c. 1748).

receive Melchizedek's blessing, while the second depicts the passage from I Samuel 21: 4-5 in which David asks the priest Ahimelech for five loaves of shewbread for his hungry soldiers.

Juan Ruiz Soriano (Higuera de la Sierra, Huelva 1701-Seville 1763), one of the most prolific artists of the first half of the century, stud-ied under Alonso Miguel de Tovar and subse-quently painted extensive series of paintings for cloisters. The Museum possesses a number of pictures from his series for the Monasteries of San Agustín – particularly important being *Our Lady of the Strap* – and San Francisco – *St Francis Receiving the Stigmata* and *St Francis Renouncing*

Domingo Martínez.
Our Lady of the Rosary (c. 1720).

Worldly Wealth. Ruiz Soriano remained true to the aesthetic ideals of the 17th century through a style deriving directly from Murillo's.

Domingo Martínez (Seville 1688-1749) was the most prominent Sevillian painter in the first half of the century. He studied under Lucas Valdés, assimilating the spirit of Murillo's work, and – due to the influence of the French painter Jean Ranc, whom he befriended when Philip V's court was at Seville (1729-1733) – gradually incorporated a French sense of aesthetics into his style.

The Museum possesses a major collection of works by Martínez, particularly important from his Murillo period being *Our Lady of the Rosary*, which is considered a copy of Murillo's original in the Dulwich Gallery, London.

Another very interesting work is his *Apotheosis of the Virgin,* a large, clearly Murillo-influenced painting in which the figure of the Virgin appears at the centre of the composition flanked by two great champions of the mystery of the Immaculate Conception – the Venerable John Duns Scotus and Sister María de Agreda. Also included in the painting are the Popes who defended the dogma of the Immaculate Conception and the Spanish kings Philip IV, Charles II and Philip V, who called for its proclamation in Rome.

Martínez's series of eight paintings known as the *Masque of the Royal Tobacco Factory*, from the Fábrica de Tabacos in Seville, is particularly interesting. They depict the carriages which paraded through the streets in 1747 to commemorate the coronation of Ferdinand VI and his wife, Bárbara de Bragança. The procession was led by the *Carriage of the Herald of the Masque*, which is depicted in front of the cathedral in the old Calle Génova. It was followed by the *Carriage of the Common Joy*, shown in front of the Archbishop's Palace on the Calle Placentines. The third carriage was the *Fire Carriage*, depicted in front of the cathedral's Door of Forgiveness. This was followed by the *Air Carriage*, with the Town Hall, the Monastery of San Francisco archway and the end of the Calle Génova behind it. The fifth was the *Water Carriage*, depicted on the corner of Alemanes and Génova streets, while the sixth, known as the *Earth Carriage*, is shown crossing the Plaza de San Francisco. The last, known as the *Carriage of the Homage of Apollo and the Three Noble Arts to the New Monarchs*, is depicted in front of the Town Hall.

The last painting illustrates *The Delivery of the Portraits of the King and Queen to the Town*

(Opposite) Juan de Espinal.
The Archangel St Michael (c. 1780).

PEDRO DE ACOSTA.
TROMPE L'OEIL (*c.* 1741).

Hall, an event which took place in front of the building.

Of evident French influence, this series was painted with extreme technical precision. Furthermore, due to Martínez's painstaking attention to detail in his depictions of the local landmarks, it is regarded as one of the finest examples of non-religious art ever produced in Spain.

Around the middle of the century the cultural influence of the Enlightenment began to reach Seville and with it the Neo-Classical spirit which was to supersede Rococo art.

Prominent in this environment was Juan de Espinal (Seville 1714-1783) – without any doubt the most representative painter of the time. Espinal studied first under his father,

Gregorio Espinal, and subsequently under Domingo Martínez. His style is a clear example of how Murillo's influence began to decline with the second generation of 18th-century painters. Espinal's work followed the predominant Rococo style of his age, which reached Spain around 1750. His own elegant, refined style and fluent, colourful strokes gave rise to the best painting produced in the Seville of the second half of the century.

Espinal was also responsible for the most important series of paintings produced in Seville at that time – a cycle of twenty-six paintings on the life of St Jerome for the cloisters of the Monastery of San Jerónimo de Buenavista in Seville. Originally semi-circular in shape, they were given their current rectangular format in the 19th century when the Museum acquired them through disentailment. Of the twenty-six paintings, the Museum possesses only ten. The rest were assigned to various churches and other museums in Seville and Huelva.

The rather inconsistent technique evident in the series (*c.* 1770-75) reveals a greater or lesser degree of participation by members of Espinal's workshop. The scenes of exteriors, in which the artist obviously took pleasure in painting landscapes in perspective, are consequently the most interesting.

A more recent acquisition is *The Archangel St Michael,* apparently a study for the version painted around 1780 for the grand staircase at the Archbishop's Palace in Seville.

The style of Pedro de Acosta's work (Seville 1690?-1756) also reveals Murillo's influence. Although the year of his birth is unknown, his work is documented from 1730 and he died in Seville in 1756. Acosta was a major exponent of the technique known in French as *trompe l'oeil*

ANDRÉS PÉREZ. *ABRAHAM BEFORE MELCHIZEDEK* (C. 1720).

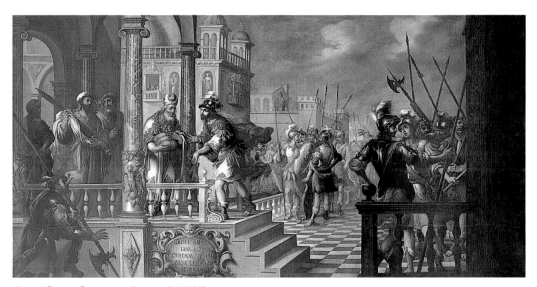

ANDRÉS PÉREZ. *DAVID BEFORE AHIMELECH* (C. 1720).

and *trampantojo* or *engañifa* in Spanish (a genre also cultivated by Murillo) whose long history began with Alonso Vázquez and Marcos Cabrera. The Museum possesses two of Acosta's *trampantojo* canvases in what was known as the "workshop corner" style. These contain what appear to be engravings of the type often used in the workshops of the age nailed onto a number of panels. Printed on both is "1741", which has enabled them to be dated.

One of the drawings in a similar painting by the Sevillian painter Diego Bejarano illustrates a *Vanitas*.

Francisco de Goya y Lucientes (Fuendetodos, Saragossa 1746 - Bordeaux 1828).

Francisco de Goya is without any doubt the most important Spanish painter of the 18th and 19th centuries and, due to the fact that his work anticipated many methods and techniques used in modern painting, the Spanish artist whose work has exerted the greatest influence on European art in general.

Born in Fuendetodos (Saragossa) in 1746, Goya lived in what was to be one of the most critical periods in European history, his lifetime spanning the whole second half of the 18th century and almost the first third of the 19th century – a period of far-reaching changes in European society and thought, deep crises and a renewal of traditional ideas and views.

Until 1780 he was best known for his decorative production, particularly his religious paintings in Saragossa and his cartoons for the Royal Santa Bárbara Tapestry Factory. However, when he discovered Velázquez's paintings in the Royal Palace between 1775 and 1778, the scope of his work increased immensely. In 1783 he produced a number of ambitious, large-format, clearly Velázquez-influenced portraits which were to prove a turning point in his work.

Goya's paintings were unknown outside Spain during his lifetime, as was the case of his prolific work and personal genius until well after the beginning of the 19th century. It was his engravings, which the Romantics would almost certainly have been acquainted with, which first brought him international acclaim.

One of the Museum's most important exhibits is Goya's magnificent portrait of canon *José Duaso y Latre* (1824), originally from the Madrid collection of Rodríguez Bavé, a relative of the sitter's. It was acquired by the Spanish state and assigned to the Museum in 1969.

Painted by Goya in his last years, this simple composition whose almost complete absence of colour emphasizes the volume and density of the brush-strokes was painted only shortly before the appearance of his "Black Paintings". In it Goya concentrated on impressing his subject's expressive power on the canvas in a faithful reflection of *Don* José's character. Goya painted this splendid canvas in gratitude to the canon for opening his doors to friends and fellow countrymen (and even to the artist himself) suspected by the authorities of harbouring liberal sympathies.

Goya is considered among the greatest portrait painters capable of capturing the personality of their sitters on canvas.

Francisco de Goya. *Canon José Duaso y Latre* (1824).

SEVILLIAN PAINTING OF THE 19TH CENTURY

• ROOMS XII AND XIII •

First Third of the Century: The Murillo Tradition.
Neo-Classicism.

Second Third: Romanticism, *Costumbrismo.*

Final Third: Historicism, Academicism and Realism.

José Villegas Cordero

Gonzalo Bilbao Martínez

• Rooms XII and XIII

The history of 19th-century art is inextricably bound up with a series of political, social and economic events – the French revolution, imperialism, the Peninsular War, liberalism, etc. – which were to leave an indelible mark upon it. An ever-increasing emphasis on the importance of work and welfare gave rise to a new social class – the bourgeoisie – which grew daily stronger and was to be the main source of the new clientele. The art of the first half of the century was dominated by Classicism and Romanticism.

On the other hand, the period between the beginning of the second half of the century and the crucial year of 1874, when the first Impressionist Exhibition was held, saw the birth of a new social force – the proletariat – and a form of social criticism which was reflected in art. Artists thus began to feel a new "commitment" to the realities of life which led to "realism" as an artistic manifestation and to "popular" trends in art.

In the course of the century Sevillian painting experienced one of its most prolific and interesting periods – a period which was to set it apart from other Spanish art schools.

Rooms XII and XIII contain paintings by the Sevillian school that are highly illustrative of the most interesting periods of the 19th century, each of which coincided with one third of that period: Neo-Classicism with its 18th-century tradition; Romanticism and *costumbrismo*; and the historicism and realism of the final third of the century.

First Third of the Century: The Murillo Tradition. Neo-Classicism

This period continued until 1833, coinciding with the reign of Ferdinand VII. At that time there were two main reasons for the general interest in copying Murillo, the first being Charles IV's predilection for the painter. When the king ordered Murillo's paintings transferred to the Royal Collection in Madrid local artists made copies to replace them. Secondly, in 1810 Marshall Soult, a great admirer of Murillo's work, plundered Seville, seizing the majority of the city's works of art, and consequently prompting the wholesale copying and imitation of Murillos by untalented local painters.

Though a minor painter, also worthy of mention in the Sevillian school of this third of the 19th century is José María Arango (Seville 1790-1883), an artist educated as a Humanist and a staunch supporter of Neo-Classicism. Although his talent as an artist can be described as somewhat limited, he was the first painter to refuse to follow Murillo's tradition, devising a completely new and original form of painting. The Museum possesses one painting by Arango; on a mythological theme, it is entitled *The Death of Pyramus and Thisbe* (c. 1830).

Second Third: Romanticism. *Costumbrismo*. (Rooms XIII to XIX)

The period between 1833 and 1868 coincided with the reign of Isabella II and a period of economic recovery which prompted a greater demand for works of art from the new clientele – the middle class. After Mendizábal's Disentailment Act of 1835, this new Sevillian social class of well-to-do families mainly from other Spanish provinces brought a new mentality to the city. With disentailment the Church ceased to be the principal client of artists and gave way to members of this new

ANTONIO MARÍA ESQUIVEL. *MRS. CARRIQUIRRE* (*c.* 1850).

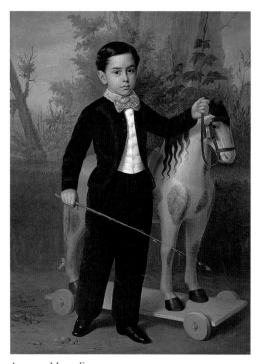

Antonio María Esquivel.
Carlos Pomar Margrand (1851).

class, many of whom subsequently rose to the ranks of the aristocracy. The change of clientele was also to prompt a change of format. As large altar paintings were no longer in demand, works of art were made considerably smaller so that they could be more easily accommodated to the mansions of the new social class. Themes also changed, the religious giving way to the profane, and the portrait, which served the middle class as a means of self-assertion, became especially important. Two types of landscape painting – urban and rural – also came into their own. Most important of all, however, was *costumbrista* painting with its folkloric features.

The Sevillian school produced the two most important Spanish Romantic painters of the

age – Antonio María Esquivel and José Gutiérrez de la Vega, who were friends and fellow-students of the same generation. Despite their very different styles, both mainly produced portraits and religious paintings.

Antonio María Esquivel (Seville 1806-1857) developed a sober style with forms severe and somewhat rigid due to the harshness of his modelling and his deep academic roots. He was active at court and became painter to Isabella II in 1843.

Despite his relatively short life Esquivel was one of the most prolific painters of the 19th century, devoting himself mainly to portraiture. He captured both the physical and psychological traits of his subjects while also paying painstaking attention to the details of their clothing.

Thanks to Andrés Siravegne's donation of 1944, the Museum possesses a large collection of Esquivel's paintings. These consist mainly of portraits, although there are also a few with religious, historical or mythological themes.

Among the great many portraits of members of the Sevillian and Madrid societies of his age is a fine *Self-portrait* (c. 1830) in which Esquivel appears to be enveloped in an atmosphere of melancholy that is typical of Romantic art. Also interesting are his portraits of the *Marquis of Peñaflorida* (1848) and the *Marquis of Bejons*. Of his portraits of women, exceptionally attractive are those of *Mrs. Carriquirre*, which clearly reflects the influence of 19th-century English painting, and *Isabella II* (1843), whom he portrayed on a number of occasions.

Of his portraits of children, *Carlos Pomar Margrand* (1851) and *Girl with a Doll* (c. 1851) best capture the tenderness and innocence of childhood. Of special interest in his work are

José Gutiérrez de la Vega.
Old Woman (*c.* 1848).

José Gutiérrez de la Vega.
Girl with a Dog (*c.* 1837).

paintings of religious themes with female nudes, depicted with dignity and decorum in a manner befitting an anatomical drawing master at the Academia de San Fernando in Madrid. Of these, *Joseph and Potiphar's Wife* (1854) and *Susanna the Chaste* (1854) both illustrate scenes from the Old Testament.

José Gutiérrez de la Vega (Seville 1791-1865) was the Spanish artist who followed most closely in Murillo's footsteps, particularly in his religious works, whose pleasing figures he painted with light, fluent brush-strokes and somewhat theatrical gestures. In his portraits the obvious influence of Goya produced a more vigorous and expressive effect.

Of the eight paintings by Gutiérrez de la Vega which belong to the Museum, six are portraits. The seventh, *St Jerome Penitent* (*c.* 1850), depicts a religious theme, while the last, enti-

tled *Murillo Exhibiting "The Colossal" Virgin of the Immaculate Conception* was acquired by the Autonomous Government of Andalusia in 1990. Through very interesting iconography it depicts the moment when the great Sevillian artist showed his finished Virgin of the Immaculate Conception to a group of ladies, gentlemen and clergymen in the Monastery of San Francisco church.

Particularly important among his portraits are those of *Fernán Caballero* (1848) and a *Girl with a Dog* (*c.* 1837).

Another prominent figure of Sevillian Romanticism was the portraitist José María Romero (Seville *c.* 1815-Madrid *c.* 1883), who, on Esquivel's and Gutiérrez de la Vega's departure from Seville, became the city's foremost portrait painter. Thanks to a series of donations, the Museum possesses five pictures he

Manuel Barrón y Carrillo. *The Cave of the Cat* (1860).

painted as official portraitist to Seville's upper-middle class and aristocracy. Particularly important among these are *José María Asensio Sánchez* and his wife *María Dolores Álvarez de Toledo*, both dating from around 1875. In order to increase the Museum's collection of Romero's work, the Autonomous Government of Andalusia acquired a *Female Nude* in 1996. This painting is noteworthy in that it is one of the few examples of nudes produced by the Spanish Romantics in general and the Sevillian Romantics in particular.

Hitherto regarded as a minor genre, landscape painting, which revealed the city's urban and rural aspects, was one of the most novel and interesting Sevillian manifestations of this period.

Its greatest exponent was Manuel Barrón (Seville 1814-1884), almost all of whose work consists of landscapes treated in a Romantic manner. Certain picturesque touches are included and human figures are ever-present.

Deeply influenced by David Roberts and the great master of Spanish Romantic landscape painting, Jenaro Pérez Villaamil (1807-1854), Barrón assimilated from both the underlying concepts of landscape painting. His small-format canvases found acceptance all over Europe.

Barrón successfully brought together all the ingredients essential to the Sevillian Romantic landscape, depicting its three different aspects – mountain, town and country. Consisting chiefly of views of Seville, his urban landscapes have become the best visual record of the city in the Romantic age.

The Museum possesses six magnificent canvases with pastoral and rural scenes by Barrón, among these *The Cave of the Cat* (1860), *Smugglers in the Ronda Mountains* (1859), *Cows Watering on the Banks of the Guadalquivir* (1860) and *Washerwomen Below Ronda* (1858).

Demand for the tired forms of Spanish "picturesque" painting – which had proved so pleasing to the tastes not only of the clientele but also to those of Romantic writers and artists all over Europe – prompted the appearance of a large school of *costumbrista* painters in Andalusia who exploited the fashion of Andalusian scenes at its very point of origin.

Whole families of painters, like the Cabral Bejaranos or the Domínguez Bécquers, dedicated themselves to this new genre. One of the best artists of this kind was Manuel Rodríguez de Guzmán (Seville 1818-Madrid 1867).

By Manuel Cabral Bejarano (Seville 1827-1891) the Museum possesses two small-format paintings entitled *Dancing in the Hall* and *Dancing in a Marquee at the Fair* which, though somewhat careless in their execution, well reflect Andalusian customs. Paintings of this kind were often sold to tourists as souvenirs.

José Domínguez Bécquer (Seville 1805-1841), the founder and father of the family, was crucial to the local art scene and devised a series of endlessly repeated prototypes. The Museum possesses his portrait of his wife *Joaquina Bastida* (*c.* 1840).

MANUEL CABRAL BEJARANO. *DANCING IN A MARQUEE AT THE FAIR*.

101

Another member of the family, Joaquín Domínguez Bécquer (Seville 1817-1879), who was José Domínguez Bécquer's cousin, also specialized in *costumbrista* scenes, although the Museum possesses only one of his portraits, that of *Manuel Moreno López* (1850).

Valeriano Domínguez Bécquer (Seville 1833-Madrid 1870), José Domínguez's son and the poet Gustavo Adolfo's brother, also specialized in portraits and *costumbrista* scenes. From his Sevillian period, the Museum possesses two highly dynamic portraits of the artists *Gumersindo Díaz* (1859) and *Francisco Tristán* painted by Valeriano Domínguez Bécquer as testimony to his friendship with them.

Painted during the Madrid period in his career, Valeriano's magnificent portrait of his brother Gustavo Adolfo (c. 1862) is considered a major work of Spanish Romantic painting. Of particular importance among his *costumbrista* paintings in this room is an *Interior of a House in Aragon* (1866) with scenes and figures typical of that Spanish region.

Final Third: Historicism. Academicism and Realism. (Rooms XII and XIII)

The final third of the 19th century spanned the fall of Isabella II in 1868, the beginning of Alfonso XIII's reign in 1886 with the regency of Maria Cristina, and fell just short of Alfonso's majority in 1902. Romanticism and *costumbrismo* died a natural death in the last years of Isabella II's reign and were succeeded by new tendencies in art – historicism, *casacón*, *preciosismo* and realism. With such diversity in the Spanish art of the late-Romantic period, the authorities created the National Fine Arts Exhibitions, a system devised to promote and at the same time control the development of the arts on a nationwide basis. Artists were encouraged to produce works illustrating historical themes, a type of art in vogue all over Europe but especially important in Spain as the authorities used it as an instrument of propaganda.

One of the artists who specialized in late-Romantic art and the new historicism was Eduardo Cano de la Peña (Seville 1823-1897), winner of the first prize at the first Exhibition, held in 1856, with his painting *Columbus at La Rábida*. Throughout his career, however, Cano continued to produce works of Romanticism, his interest in historicism due more to the dictates of fashion than to a true sense of vocation.

Of Eduardo Cano's paintings the Museum possesses two with historical themes: *The Catholic Monarchs Receiving Christian Captives at the Conquest of Malaga* (1867) and *Friar with the Head of Álvaro de Luna* (1892), in which a Capuchin friar holds the head of the executed Constable in his hands.

Cano also produced genre paintings and portraits, particularly interesting from this second type being a portrait of the poetess *Fernán Caballero* (c. 1870).

By 1875 most of the great figures of Romantic painting were dead, the market was glutted with paintings of scenes of dancing in inns and fairs, Andalusian society was changing, and Meissonier's Neo-Romantic *tableautin* was in vogue all over Europe.

The combined influence of the *tableautin* and the Goyesque was to characterize the early period in the career of the great renovator of Spanish Restoration painting, Mariano Fortuny.

(Opposite) Valeriano Domínguez Bécquer. *Gustavo Adolfo Bécquer* (c. 1862).

In turn, Fortuny's influence was to be crucial to Andalusian Neo-Romanticism, although in this respect the influence of the Italian and French painting of the period should also be taken into account, for, thanks to official bodies like the Seville Council, many painters of this generation travelled to Rome or Paris to acquaint themselves with the prevalent trends.

Of this generation was José Jiménez Aranda (Seville 1837-1903), who moved to Rome in 1871, where he met Fortuny and took an interest in the type of painting known in Spain as *casacón*, a version of 18th-century *costumbrista* scenes whose name was derived from the custom of depicting the figures in dress coats (*casacas*) and wigs, etc. Jiménez Aranda returned to Seville in 1875, but turned back to *casacón* in 1881 when, on a visit to Paris, he assimilated Meissonier's style so thoroughly that he became one of the main Spanish painters of the theme. Nevertheless, a journey to Madrid in 1890 inclined him to Realism, a movement prevalent in the Spanish painting of the last decade of the century, one example of his work being *A Misfortune*. In 1892 he again returned to Seville where, without completely abandoning *casacón*, he concentrated on portraiture, landscape (joining the group of Alcalá de Guadaira *plein air* painters) and above all anecdotal paintings.

Of his prolific production, the Museum possesses only portraits, one being of his daughter *Irene* (1889) against a neutral background free of decorative conventions, centring the attention on the girl's personality. Also exhibited is a *Self-portrait* (*c.* 1870).

José García Ramos (Seville 1852-1912) was a disciple and friend of José Jiménez Aranda, with whom he travelled to Rome. There he also met Fortuny, the result of their encounter being a large number of *casacón* paintings. He also produced many pictures of *bandoleros* and *majos* of past ages as well as scenes from everyday life in Seville, from bullfighting to flamenco celebrations. His grace and wit have made him one of the foremost representatives of the Sevillian *costumbrismo* of the late 19th century. Of special interest in the Museum are *Dancing Partners* (*c.* 1885), *Bulerias* (1884), for which he won the gold medal at the 1884 Seville Exhibition, *The Boy with a Violin* (*c.* 1905) and *Malvaloca* (1912), named after the main character from one of the Álvarez Quintero brothers' most popular plays.

Emilio Sánchez Perrier (Seville 1855-Alhama de Granada 1907), who studied at the Academia de Bellas Arts in Seville under Joaquín Domínguez Bécquer and Eduardo Cano, was the foremost landscape painter of his time. Through his various trips to Paris he became acquainted with French Realist landscape painting and was influenced by Corot and the Barbizon school, whose style is characterized by motifs constantly found in Sánchez Perrier's landscapes – groves, river banks, ponds, etc. He is considered one of the most important figures in the history of landscape painting and his influence was essential to the appearance of Sevillian Realist landscape painting. He is also regarded as the founder of the Alcalá de Guadaira school, one example of his work of that time being *Pine Woods at Alcalá de Guadaira*. His work also includes views of Seville and its river, as in *Triana*, exhibited in this room, which in addition to its great importance as a work of art, serves as a valuable record of a view of the river flowing through Triana, a district that has since changed considerably.

(Opposite) José García Ramos. *"Bulerias"* (*c.* 1884).

José Jiménez Aranda.
Irene Jiménez (1889).

José Lafita (Jerez de la Frontera 1855-Seville 1925), another prominent member of the Alcalá de Guadaira school, painted many Guadalquivir riverbank scenes set in both the city and the country. One fine example in the Museum is *Alcalá de Guadaira Landscape* (*c.* 1900).

Rafael Senet (Seville 1856-1926) studied under Joaquín Domínguez Bécquer and Eduardo Cano. In 1881 he travelled to Italy, staying in Rome, Venice and Naples, where he associated with the Portici group. His famous *vedute* paintings of Venice proved highly successful. In 1890 he returned to Seville, where he concentrated on landscape painting, thanks to his association with Sánchez Perrier and García Rodríguez, with whom he painted in

the area around Alcalá de Guadaira. From his Italian period the Museum possesses *Doge's Palace* (Rome 1887), *Venetian Canal* (Venice 1885) and *The Fisherwoman* (Rome 1885).

Andrés Parladé (Malaga 1859-Seville 1933) studied painting in Malaga under Moreno Carbonero. He travelled to Paris and subsequently to Rome, living there from 1883 to 1891, when he returned to Seville. He was elected academician at the Academia de Bellas Artes in 1902. His first paintings clearly reflect the historicist academicism of the Rome of the final third of the 19th century. When historicism came to an end he turned to *costumbrismo*, developing a fluent, energetic technique. Parladé was particularly proficient at depicting animals, especially dogs and horses. Thanks to a donation made by his widow in 1945, the Museum possesses a large selection of his work, including *Woman and White Dog* (1899) and *Self-portrait as a Hunter* (1907). He also produced a number of exceptional paintings of *majas* and bullfighters, among these *The Injured Bullfighter* and *Bullfighter on a Bench*. A large collection of works of this type has been on display at the Museo de Artes y Costumbres Populares in Seville since its inauguration in 1973.

José Arpa (Carmona, Seville 1860-Seville 1952) was a pupil of Eduardo Cano's. In 1883 he won a Seville Council scholarship to travel to Rome and there he met José Villegas Cordero. He embarked on his career with historical themes but subsequently turned to landscape painting, a genre in which he proved himself a master due to his bold use of colour and light and his direct view of nature. In 1896 he journeyed to the Americas, living in Mexico and Texas. Among the results of his stay there

EMILIO SÁNCHEZ PERRIER. *Triana* (*c.* 1888-90).

are *The Grand Canyon, Arizona* (*c.* 1925) and a magnificent landscapes full of colour and light entitled *Flowering Prickly Pears* (*c.* 1928).

José Rico Cejudo (Seville 1864-1939) studied under José García Ramos. He travelled to Rome in 1888 on a Seville Council grant. A large part of his work is devoted to detailed reconstructions of 18th-century Seville featuring *précieux* processions, weddings and interiors. He was well-known for his Venetian landscapes but mainly produced scenes with figures of flower sellers, flamenco dancers and priests from the Seville of his time, one fine example being *Flower Sellers in María Luisa Park* (*c.* 1920).

Ricardo López Cabrera (Cantillana, Seville 1864-Seville 1950) studied under Eduardo Cano and José Jiménez (whose son-in-law he later became). In 1887 he travelled on a Seville Council grant to Rome, where he moved with-in strictly academicist circles, as is evident in the Museum's *The Gladiator* (1888). His work displays a wide variety of themes from *costumbrista casacóns* to landscapes and portraits. Particularly interesting among this last type are the portraits of *Casilda López de Haro* (1889) and her husband *Fernando Antón de Olmet* (1891), both donated to the Museum by the Marquis of Dos Fuentes in 1955.

Another artist whose work is exhibited here is Nicolás Jiménez Alperiz (Seville 1865-1928), a specialist in small-format paintings depicting a multitude of *costumbrista* aspects of Sevillian life. The Museum possesses his *Story of Witches* (*c.* 1910), a *Self-portrait* and a portrait of *Germán Repetto* (1924). He was also a painter of historical themes but as a member of the Alcalá de Guadaira school also produced landscapes, one of his most interesting being a *View of Seville Cathedral from the Guadalquivir* (1893).

107

Rafael Senet. *Venetian Canal* (1885).

Fernando Tirado (Seville 1862-1907) studied under Eduardo Cano and travelled to Paris on a Seville Council grant in 1878. Although he mainly painted portraits, he also produced Arabic themes and *costumbrista* scenes. His work is represented in the Museum by two paintings: a portrait of *Queen Maria Cristina and Her Son Alfonso XIII* (1891) and an Arabic theme entitled *Moorish Ambush* (1880).

Francisco Narbona (Seville 1861-*c.* 1920) moved to Rome in 1887, studying there under José Villegas and becoming an exponent of historicism. The Museum possesses *Samaritan Woman* (1889), a painting from his Rome period which clearly reflects his academicist training.

Another academicist painter was Domingo Fernández (Seville 1862-*c.* 1920) who won a scholarship in 1886 to study in Rome. From this period is *Leda and the Swan* (Rome 1888).

He spent most of the rest of his career in Argentina, where he painted works of *costumbrismo*.

The foremost artists in Seville during this period were José Villegas Cordero and Gonzalo Bilbao.

José Villegas Cordero
(Seville 1844-Madrid 1921)

In Italy, Villegas Cordero was regarded as the Spanish artist second only to Fortuny. He studied first at the workshop of the painter José María Romero and subsequently at the Escuela de Bellas Artes in Seville. In 1866 he moved to Madrid, where he studied the great masters of 17th-century naturalism at the Prado Museum, particularly Velázquez, from whom he took the

NICOLÁS JIMÉNEZ ALPERIZ. *VIEW OF SEVILLE CATHEDRAL FROM THE GUADALQUIVIR* (1893).

basis of his pictorial technique. He frequented Federico de Madrazo's studio, where he met Fortuny. He left Madrid for Rome with Luis Jiménez Aranda and Francisco Peralta at the end of 1868.

In the Italian capital he took Rosales's old studio and attended evening classes at the famous Chigi academy. This period was followed by his most prosperous years as an artist (as Fortuny's most dedicated follower) during which he supplied an international clientele willing to pay high prices for his work and won a succession of prizes at international exhibitions. In his historical paintings he strove for the highest degree of naturalism while paying special attention to detail in the settings.

From 1877 his various stays in Venice proved especially useful to his *costumbrista* works with Venetian architectural backgrounds and to his

historical paintings, examples of the latter being · *The Triumph of the Dogaressa* (1892) and *The Doge Mocenigo*. These paintings reflect his deep interest in the Italian Renaissance and his knowledge of the Quattrocento and Cinquecento masters – another fine example being *Palm Sunday in Venice*. As a Spaniard in Rome he had a great deal of success with Spanish *costumbrista* scenes, particularly of bullfights.

Evident in other Italian-inspired works of his are elegant, undulating lines and an expressive idiom derived from Botticelli. A prolific artist, he also produced landscapes, portraits and *casacón* paintings. His career in Rome reached its peak with his appointment as Director of the Academia Española in 1898. On his return to Spain in 1901 he was appointed Director of the Museo del Prado. In 1914 he began work on an ambitious series of twelve art nouveau-

José Villegas.
The Sculptor Ercole Monty (c. 1875).

of which are portraits, are paintings of *The Sculptor Ercole Monty* (*c.* 1875), *Luz Ojeda* (*c.* 1910), Villegas's wife *Lucía Monty* (*c.* 1915) and a self-portrait *I, Villegas* (*c.* 1875-76).

Villegas's *costumbrista* paintings were extremely successful. One of the most important is *The Death of the Master* (*c.* 1910), which now forms part of the Museum's collection. Based on the typically Spanish theme of bullfighting, it won him international fame and prestige through its moving depiction of the mem-

José Villegas.
Luz Ojeda (c. 1906).

and symbolist-influenced canvases entitled *The Decalogue of Life* consisting of the Ten Commandments with a prologue and epilogue.

Thanks to a donation from his widow, Lucía Monty, the Museum has possessed a major collection of Villegas's work since 1921. Particularly interesting among these works, most

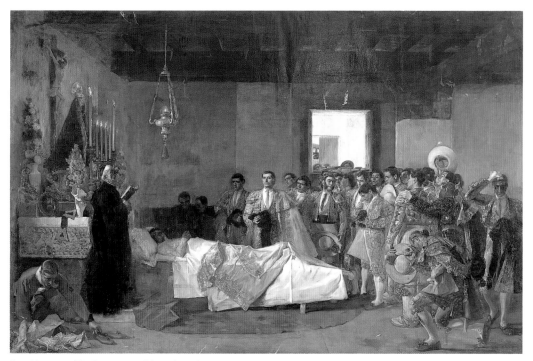

JOSÉ VILLEGAS. *THE DEATH OF THE MASTER* (1910).

bers of Bocanegra's team gathered at the bull-fighter's bedside in the bullring's infirmary, where he was taken after being fatally gored by a bull.

Villegas's long career spanned the prevalent trends of the last third of the 19th and early years of the 20th centuries. He moved from the Realism of Rosales to the preciosity of Fortuny to finally produce works closely associated with Impressionism and Symbolism.

Gonzalo Bilbao Martínez
(Seville 1860-Madrid 1938)

On the threshold between the 19th and 20th centuries, Andalusian painting fully entered the spirit of the ideas of renewal marked by French Impressionism as represented in Spain by the light-saturated works of Sorolla.

Gonzalo Bilbao was the pioneer of the new luminist *costumbrismo* and a key figure in the Sevillian school at the turn of the 19th century.

He received his early training at the workshop of the de Vega brothers, Francisco and Pedro, and in 1880 went to Rome to continue his studies at José Villegas's workshop. He moved to Paris in 1883 and in 1887 entered his painting *Daphnis and Chloe* for the National Fine Arts Exhibition prize, coming second. In 1888 he travelled to Morocco, where he painted *Slaves on a Terrace*, for which he won third prize at the Paris National Exhibition in 1889. He then settled permanently in Seville and

GONZALO BILBAO. *MAIN CLOISTER OF THE MONASTERY OF LA MERCED IN SEVILLE* (*c.* 1920).

became one of the most brilliant representatives of regionalist *costumbrismo*. In 1925 he was elected Chairman of the Academia de Santa Isabel de Hungría.

One of Bilbao's greatest preoccupations (and ultimately one of his greatest successes) was the use of light, and in its pursuit his technique came close to that of the French Impressionists. His work is easily distinguished by his expert lines, great compositional skill and rich colour range.

Extremely varied, his themes range from portraiture and landscape to scenes of Andalusian customs, interpreted with a deep sense of realism drawn from life itself. Everyday life in Seville and the surrounding countryside, the hard work of the reapers and cigar-makers, were all transferred to his canvas with a sincerity which on occasions bordered on social criticism.

Particularly important among the Museum's large collection of Bilbao's work is *The Cigarmakers* (1915). The anecdotal motif of these women at work served Bilbao for a study of perspective and light effects resulting in one of his best compositions.

His works of *costumbrismo* are represented in the Museum by *Summer Night in Seville* (1905).

GONZALO BILBAO. *THE CIGAR-MAKERS* (1915).

Although there are few nudes in Gonzalo Bilbao's work, *La toilette* (*c.* 1910) served him as a pretext for a superficial treatment of the theme, despite which the painting is principally a study of light.

Particularly interesting among his portraits are those of *Francisco Rodríguez Marín* (1934) and *José Gestoso* (1914), as well as two members of his family, his sister *Flora* (1914) and his wife *María Roy* (1926).

His landscape painting in its various aspects is represented in the Museum by *Marina* (1928), *Zocodover Square* (1910) and *Main Cloister of the Monastery of La Merced in Seville* (1920).

Bilbao's work proves him to be the founder of the early 20th-century Sevillian school where the masters Miguel Angel del Pino, Gustavo Bacarisas, Javier de Winthuysen, Santiago Martínez and Alfonso Grosso all received their training.

20TH-CENTURY PAINTING

• ROOM XIV •

The Sevillian School

Other Schools

• ROOM XIV

This room contains a small exhibition of paintings representing the Sevillian and other Spanish schools of the first half of the 20th century.

The Sevillian School

The Sevillian painting of this period displays a number of special characteristics. The avant-garde movements such as Cubism, Fauvism, Expressionism, etc., were almost completely ignored by the Sevillian painters of this generation.

These painters were great enthusiasts of the artistic values identified with Sevillian tradition and Andalusian regionalism, which prompted the appearance of a superficial, anecdotal form of painting of clear Romantic influence depicting *costumbrista* scenes of gypsies, flamenco dancers, altar boys and peasants. Although some painters also displayed a commitment to social realism, they did so more in an attempt to attract the attention of the jury at the National Exhibitions than to meet the demands of their customers.

Despite this rather parochial attitude in the Sevillian art of the first half of the 20th century, three painters either born or trained in Seville broke away from the conventions of 19th-century painting, although it would be an exaggeration to describe them as avant-garde.

Gustavo Bacarisas (Gibraltar 1873-Seville 1971) was a cosmopolitan painter. He travelled to Rome and Paris and in 1914, in the prime of life and at the height of his career, settled permanently in Seville, a city which not only pro-vided him with colour and light for his paintings but also with a way of living and thinking he found highly attractive.

Bacarisas was an artist who, although influenced by the painting of the previous century, went one step further and created a very personal style clearly based on Art Nouveau with Impressionist influences and above all on Fauvism.

He was particularly fond of painting night-time scenes, endowing them with an underlying atmosphere of deep lyricism. He depicted a large assortment of themes from Andalusian life, including gypsies, bullfighters, flamenco dancers, etc.

Exhibited in this room is his *Feast Day in Seville* (1915), donated to the Museum by the Seville traders' association in 1939. In it Bacarisas displayed the elegance and colourfulness characteristic of his style throughout his career. This painting is, in short, a poem to the grace and beauty of Sevillian women.

Javier Winthuysen (Seville 1874-Barcelona 1956) received his training at his master Gonzalo Bilbao's workshop. In 1903 he travelled to Paris and discovered Impressionism. In 1912 he settled in Madrid, where, influenced by his Paris experience, he studied landscape gardening. As a specialist in this field he laid out and redesigned noteworthy gardens all over Spain, facets of his activity which ultimately led him to paint both town and country landscapes.

The high quality of his painting lies with classicism and an enveloping use of light, colours appearing as illuminated forms. His highly poetic landscapes reflect nature precisely as he perceived it.

The Museum has possessed a large collection of landscapes and portraits by Winthuysen since

GUSTAVO BACARISAS. *FEAST DAY IN SEVILLE* (1915).

1980, thanks to a donation by his daughter Salud. The portraits display deep psychological insight into the subjects and confident, precise lines of high technical quality. Particularly interesting is a *Self-portrait* painted in 1920 in which the painter captured his own elegance and deep spirituality.

The painting exhibited in this room, entitled *Entrance to the Ceperos Gardens*, is a fine example of the features typical of Winthuysen's art.

Winthuysen can be described as an upholder of tradition, for through his works the elements typical of the Sevillian garden, the Generalife

117

ponds, and the gardens of Aranjuez, among others, have lived on.

Alfonso Grosso (Seville 1893-1983) studied under García Ramos and Gonzalo Bilbao, the influence of both remaining evident in all his subsequent work. Through the former he acquired a taste for regionalist themes and through the latter his use of colour and a predilection for effects of light.

Rejecting the European avant-garde movements, Grosso remaining true to the academicist and traditional, his only concession to modernity being the adoption of certain Impressionist postulates. He took part in a number of National Exhibitions and in 1920 won third prize for his *The Altar Boy* (1920).

In 1942 he was appointed Director of the Museo Provincial de Bellas Artes in Seville, a post he held until 1969. His years at the Museum were to influence his art and he was deeply inspired by the work of the great Sevillian Baroque painter Francisco Zurbarán.

His themes are extremely varied – urban landscapes, gardens, customs, figures, *bodegones* and interiors. This last field was his favourite due to the influence of his master, Gonzalo Bilbao, whose *The Cigar-makers* (1915) made a deep impression on him and served as a basis for his intimist compositions. His interiors are never uninhabited as he considered the presence of human figures indispensable.

Grosso took the personages in his paintings – gypsy girls, bullfighters, flamenco dancers, etc. – from life. Unlike his master, García Ramos, who invented his characters, Grosso painted real portraits of already famous people.

The Museum possesses five works donated by the artist himself during his period as Director.

Particularly important are *The Altar Boy* (1920), *The Novice's Communion* (*c.* 1930) and *The Museum's Patrons* (1951).

Generally speaking, Grosso's paintings reflect a sense of gaiety devoid of drama though not of feeling.

Santiago Martínez (Villaverde del Rio, Seville 1890-Seville 1979) studied under García Ramos and Gonzalo Bilbao, adding to their influence the knowledge he acquired of Sorolla's painting in Madrid. His style displays a restrained form of Impressionism endowed with a special sense of light and colour. His work is represented in this room by *Avila Landscape* (1955).

Other painters from this time worthy of mention and represented in the Museum are: Miguel Angel del Pino (Seville 1890-1973), Manuel González Santos (Seville 1875-1949), Juan Rodríguez Jaldón (Osuna, Seville 1890-Seville 1967) and José María Labrador (Benamejí, Córdoba 1891–Nerva 1971).

Other Schools

A regionalist painter of southern Spain from the Granada school, José María Rodríguez Acosta (Granada 1878-1941) distinguished himself through his interpretation of gypsy themes, treating them with credibly serious and deeply sentimental realism. Official acceptance of this genre led to him winning first prize at the 1908 National Fine Arts Exhibition with *Gypsies of Sacromonte* (1908).

The Granada painter who most faithfully represents this regionalist school is Francisco Soria Aedo (Granada 1898-Madrid 1965), who studied under Muñoz Lucena and López Mezquita. His work consists mainly of crowded *costum-*

brista paintings, portraits, symbolist compositions and pagan and Arabic scenes.

Thanks to a donation by the Marchioness of Távara, the Museum's collection of Soria Aedo's work has recently increased with a painting entitled *Young Girl with Mantilla and Bullfighters*.

Eugenio Hermoso (Fregenal de la Sierra, Badajoz, 1883-Madrid, 1963) belonged to the generation of Extremadura painters of the turn of the century who, in the wake of the succession of traditional idioms of most Spanish regions in the second half of the 19th century, represent the trends of *costumbrista* regionalism in the 20th century. The Museum possesses various of this artist's works, including *Rosa*, for which he won second prize at the 1908 National Exhibition in Madrid, and *Village Piety* (1908), one of several paintings donated by his heirs in 1999.

Daniel Vázquez Díaz (Nerva, Huelva 1882-Madrid 1969) moved from his native Huelva to Seville in 1892 to study art, often visiting the Museo de Pinturas, where the work of two great masters – Zurbarán and El Greco – made a deep impression on him. From Zurbarán's last years in particular come the silvery lights, the whites and pinks, the monumentality and the severity of figures so typical of Vázquez Díaz's work. He was particularly impressed by El Greco's portrait of his son Jorge Manuel, in which the painter captured the potential of intense, refined colour.

It was also in Seville where he met the great Basque painter Ignacio Zuloaga, who by them had settled in the city. At this time and due to Zuloaga's influence, he began to paint bullfighting scenes, a favourite theme throughout his career.

In 1903 he moved to Madrid, where he met Juan Gris and entered various National Exhibitions. In 1906 he travelled to Paris, where

DANIEL VÁZQUEZ DÍAZ.
THE "CUADRILLA" OF JUAN CENTENO (1953).

he and Amedeo Modigliani met and became great friends. It was during his stay in Paris when he was first attracted to Impressionism, a movement which the artists of his circle had by then abandoned. The ten paintings exhibited by Cézanne at the 1906 Salon d'Automne proved decisive to his training. The sense of volume, monumentality and sobriety were the features he most admired in the French painter's work.

Vázquez Díaz produced many fine portraits of contemporary celebrities and friends, including Rubén Darío, Unamuno, Juan Ramón Jiménez, the Baroja brothers and even the king, Alfonso XIII. In the course of these years he alternated his place of residence between Paris and Madrid.

At the National Exhibition of 1915 he entered *The Death of the Bullfighter*, also entitled *Pain*, a well-organized, severe and monumental composition displaying alternating brilliant and sober shades of colour.

In the course of his career he entered a large number of National Exhibitions, but did not win a "Medal of Honour" until 1953, when he was finally awarded the coveted prize for *The Cuadrilla of Juan Centeno*, a work characteristic of his technique and style that is full of expressiveness, colour and monumentality.

His aesthetic ideology was based on both the ancient and the modern: Zurbarán and Cézanne.

By the Huelva-born painter Sebastián García Vázquez (Puebla de Guzmán 1904-1989) the Museum possesses a *costumbrista* painting entitled *The Woodcutters* (1948).

The pessimistic view of Spanish life in the early years of the 20th century was presented in literature by the Generation of '98, while in painting it was interpreted by the great internationally-famous Basque portraitist Ignacio Zuloaga (Eibar 1870-Madrid 1945). Closely associated with Seville for several years, Zuloaga and other contemporary painters depicted the somewhat sordid and dramatic austerity of the Spanish character both in their portraits and their paintings of bullfighters and marginalized regional types.

Exhibited in this room is Zuloaga's portrait of *The Painter Uranga*, a picture of extreme realism dating from 1931 and loaned to the Museum in 1973 by the Museo de Arte Contemporáneo de Madrid, now the Museo Nacional Centro de Arte Reina Sofía.

One of the most representative figures of 20th-century Spanish figurative art is the Castilian-born Antonio Ortiz Echagüe (Guadalajara 1883-Buenos Aires 1942), a member of the generation of painters born in the last third of the 19th century who called for a return to the art of everyday life as opposed to academicism. Thus a popular or *costumbrista* style of Realism appeared which had more in common with the Spanish Golden Age than Courbet. Generally speaking it can be described as Post-Impressionist, coming ever closer to the decorative aspects of Art Nouveau and the bold colour and gesture typical of the Fauves and the first Expressionists.

However, despite influences, Ortiz Echagüe was his own painter, with a personal artistic idiom suffused at one and the same time with tradition and modernity. His varied themes – popular figures, domestic scenes, interiors, landscapes, etc. – reflect a pleasant, contented image of existence and he never depicted dramatic themes. His painting is figurative and naturalistic, but the people he depicts are not conventional, for they are filled with a deep inner life.

His canvas *Dutch Interior* (1920; on loan from the Museo Nacional Centro de Arte Reina Sofía) displays all the features typical of his work. Painted in the Dutch town of Arnemuiden, it is full of extraordinary realism.

IGNACIO ZULOAGA. *THE PAINTER URANGA* (1931).

Drawings

The Museum's collection of drawings forms an important part of its holdings. Its interest lies not only in its large size – 632 items – but also in the variety of techniques – watercolour, charcoal, ink, sanguine, wax, etc. – it displays. The vast majority were executed by 19th-century Sevillian artists whose paintings are also displayed in the Museum's exhibition rooms and for whom drawing was a crucial phase in each new work. This was particularly true in the case of Antonio María Esquivel, José Jiménez Aranda, Gonzalo Bilbao and José García Ramos.

In addition to this main group (on loan to the Museum from the Real Academia de Bellas Artes de Santa Isabel de Hungría in Seville), a number of other drawings have come from private donations, such as those made by Andrés Siravegne in 1944 and Lucia Monty in 1922. The latter consists of sixteen paintings and various other items in addition to almost six hundred drawings – all by her husband, the painter José Villegas Cordero – which are indispensable to a knowledge of the work of one of the most important Sevillian artists of the 19th century.

Chronologically, the first drawings – several half-length portraits by Francisco Cabral Bejarano (1824-1890) and a group portrait by Antonio María Esquivel (1806-1857) of artists gathered in his workshop – date from the Romantic age. These are small-format works whose main virtue lies in the accurate, detailed lines which perfectly capture the middle-class society of the times in the same way as the artists' pictures. Careful attention to detail in the treatment of the subject is also the main feature in the watercolours of the Seville chronicler Joaquín Guichot y Parodi (1820-1890), whose *Drawings of Monuments, Views and Curiosities of Seville* are a valuable record of a number of the city's streets and buildings.

Costumbrismo was practised by a large number of Sevillian artists and faithful reflections of this movement with its typical figures and pleasant scenes are *Indian Summer* (1898) by José García Ramos (1852-1912), *Portrait of a Gentleman* by Joaquín Turina y Areal (1847-1903), and *Gypsy Girl* and *Dozing Soldier* both by Gonzalo Bilbao (1860-1938).

Rafael Senet's (1856-1926) watercolours display an "orientalist" tendency, fine examples of his work being *Moorish Girl Playing the Cymbals* (1881) and *Moor with Musket* (1882). The latter is quite startling due to its colour, variety and the realism of the figure, his clothing and the objects around him.

As mentioned above, the most important drawings are the work of the painter José Villegas Cordero (1844-1921), who was one of the greatest exponents of historical painting. This is evident in his preparatory sketches for *Social Peace in Venice* which illustrates an important event in the history of the Venetian Republic. Two main characteristics are immediately apparent in the drawings: first, and as is customary in historical painting, the importance attached by the artist to the subject, the narrative and the setting; and second Villegas Cordero's technique, which is highly reminis-

José Villegas. *Sketch for the Cortège of Ladies from The Triumph of the Dogaressa* (1892).

cent of the Florentine Renaissance artists he had studied during his stay in Rome. Thus, the line becomes the basic element of these drawings in which with extreme meticulousness the artist provided a detailed description of the main figures – besides the retinue, pages, functionaries and musicians – and the architectural setting. Also from his stay in Italy are a number of landscapes whose fluent, expressive technique perfectly captures the atmosphere of the Venice of the age.

On his return to Spain in 1901, he received several commissions, including illustrations for *Don Quixote*, sketches for banknotes for the Bank of Spain (1902) and the *Allegory of Seville* album for the Real Maestranza (1906). However, there is no doubt that his most important project was *Decalogue of Life* (1898-1914), which can be considered representative of his entire production. From this series of twelve paintings, the Museum possesses a large number of sketches and preliminary drawings which reveal a vivid imagination. These compositions are highly symbolist in character as their forms and images served Villegas Cordero as a vehicle for deep meditation on concepts such as love, life, evil and death. The importance he placed on landscape and the colour and light enveloping his scenes underline that deep spiritual reflection.

Also exhibited are collections of ceramics, gold- and silverwork, weapons, embroidery, furniture and documents, all of unquestionable value and high artistic quality and perfectly illustrative of the variety of types and development of forms from the Middle Ages to the 20th century.

Regarding the number of exhibits and their artistic importance, a clear distinction can be drawn between the precious metal and ceramics collections and the others, as the Sevillian school has a long, distinguished tradition in gold- and silverwork and an even longer one in ceramics.

Unlike the Museum's painting and sculpture, only some of the ceramic panels were acquired (1868) as a result of disentailment. The other collections increased in the course of the 20th century thanks to private donations, the most important of these being the Gestoso (1912), González Abreu (1918), Soria (1924) and Aguiar (1945) donations.

Ceramics

The collection of ceramics includes tiles, panels and individual pieces of chinaware. Most of the panels came from the walls of Sevillian monasteries, but on their acquisition by the Museum with the disentailment of 1868, they came to grace the walls of the building's various courts.

The oldest items are fragments of Arabic-style tiles with geometrical motifs, a type superseded at the end of the 15th century by another made with the *cuerda seca* method and yet later by a more advanced technique with contributions by artists. This last type incorporated decorative elements such as vegetal motifs and heraldic emblems.

The most important innovation in this field came during the Renaissance with Francesco Niculoso Pisano, an Italian artist who set up a workshop in Triana and transformed the ceramics produced in Seville in two special ways. First he introduced technical advances based on the new majolica earthenware, producing smooth, painted tiles, henceforth known in Seville as "Pisano" or "Italiano" which could be combined with others to form large compositions. Second, he increased decorative themes with the introduction of truly Renaissance-style scenes, forms and elements such as adornment with grotesques, cartouches and wreaths. A third characteristic of his work is Flemish influence, evident above all where attention to detail is concerned. The Patio del Aljibe contains a number of panels from Pisano's workshop depicting *God the Father and the Emblems of the Four Evangelists* (*c.* 1525). In these the figures are accentuated by a fine black outline and display a bright, vivid range of blues, yellows, oranges and whites that are typical of his work.

By Cristóbal de Augusta, *Our Lady of the Rosary* was signed and dated in 1577 and came originally from the Convent of Madre de Dios in Seville. Almost certainly inspired by a picture by the Sevillian painter Luis de Vargas, it depicts Our Lady of Mercy protecting Dominican cler-

CRISTÓBAL DE AUGUSTA. *OUR LADY OF THE ROSARY* (1577).

ics. Zurbarán was later to paint a similar scene for the Carthusians.

The most important workshop in the city during the first half of the 17th century was that of the Valladares family, whose most prominent member, Hernando, continued Pisano's style in his decoration of pilasters, friezes and frontals. The Museum possesses various examples of his work, one being the frame surrounding the door to the Patio del Aljibe (*c.* 1600), originally from

125

the Monastery of San Pablo. It is adorned with putti, animals, and shields. Another example is the frontal of the altar dedicated to Saints Justa and Rufina (*c.* 1600) in the Patio de los Bojes. Originally from the former Monastery of La Anunciación in Seville, it depicts the saints with their traditional iconography surrounded by profuse naturalist decoration. Also attributed to Hernando de Valladares is the decoration of the Main Cloister of the former Monastery of La Merced, now the site of this Museum.

As the 17th century advanced and the Sevillian Baroque school reached its height, the pictorial type of decoration in ceramics became ever more popular, prompting the large devotional series which adorned the altarpiece-façades of monasteries and convents. That at Santa Maria del Popolo (*c.* 1670) consisted of two central panels flanked by figures of saints and bishops. The first, of *St Ambrose of Milan*, is now in the lobby, while the other, *Our Lady of Santa Maria del Popolo*, is in the Patio de los Bojes.

Another example of Baroque pictorial tilework decoration in the Patio is *Our Lady of the Immaculate Conception Surrounded by Nuns and Angels* (*c.* 1680-1700). This pictorial tradition continued during the 18th century, as is evident in the panel of *Christ Helped by Simon of Cyrene*, (*c.* 1770), originally from the St Philip Neri arch and now in the lobby.

The Museum's other large group of ceramics consists of household chinaware (plates, pitchers and trays) and pharmacy jars, most of which have been on loan to the Museo de Artes y Costumbres Populares since 1972. In addition to the collection of Sevillian Baroque chinaware are pieces from other important workshops in Spain – Talavera, Manises and Alcora – and also from abroad – Italy (Faenza, Genoa, Savona),

Germany and Portugal. Also important is the Museum's collection of plates, pitchers and pharmacy jars made by José Gestoso at the beginning of the 20th century according to the mediaeval *cuerda seca* technique. It was donated to the Museum by his widow in 1912.

Gold- and Silverwork

The Museum's collection of gold- and silverwork consists of fifty-nine items, mainly from the González Abreu (1928) donation, which trace the development of religious and profane pieces made with these precious metals from the Gothic period to the present day. Although the most important group of items are the trays, there is also an assortment of chalices, crowns, jugs, censers, ostensories, pyxes, etc.

Only three of the pieces are Gothic: a bust-reliquary (13th-14th century), part of a processional cross, and a 16th-century censer (exhibited with a portable stoup of painted glass also dating from the 16th century).

In the course of the 16th century ornamentation changed and Renaissance and Mannerist elements began to be incorporated. From the late Renaissance period (last third of the 16th century) are a processional cross, a small chest and a cup, all of which, like the Gothic pieces, lack marks of any kind, making identification of their origin virtually impossible. However, most of these pieces are similar to others then made all over Spain, including Andalusia.

The advent of Mannerism (which continued until well after the beginning of the 17th century) saw the appearance of a trend in geometrical ornamentation, as can be seen in the three typically Spanish lipped jugs on display. In two of

Hᴇʀɴᴀɴᴅᴏ ᴅᴇ Vᴀʟʟᴀᴅᴀʀᴇs. *Dᴏᴏʀ sᴜʀʀᴏᴜɴᴅ* (*ᴄ.* 1600).

127

these, austere decoration surrounds the handle and lip.

The Baroque age was a time of splendour for European silverwork, as is evident from one of the Museum's most important items, which came from the Marquis of Blanco Hermoso's collection and was acquired by the Government of Andalusia in 1988. Of plain and gilded silver and crystal, it depicts Neptune driving a chariot drawn by sea horses emerging from the water and accompanied by human and animal figures. This piece displays features heralding Baroque art, as for example the dynamism and expressiveness of the group, which is treated in a sculptural manner.

The most important collection of 17th-century silver items consists of trays. Seville had always been Spain's foremost silversmithing centre but as the century advanced Córdoba slowly began to displace it. From the Córdoba school the Museum possesses three silver trays, one by the well-known smith Damián de Castro. In all three, highly dynamic naturalist vegetal motif relief covers the whole surface.

As in other artistic fields, the Rococo style became predominant under the Bourbons and the introduction of rocaille prompted a change in the decorative aspects of gold- and silverwork.

ANONYMOUS. *NEPTUNE'S CHARIOT* (*SALTCELLAR*). 17TH CENTURY.

Tray. (Second half of the 18th century).

The 19th century began with Neo-Classicism, which gave way to other "new" styles – Neo-Gothic, Neo-Renaissance, Neo-Mannerist, Neo-Baroque and Neo-Rococo. The exhibits reveal how the models and types of adornment of previous periods were simply copied without innovation until the advent of Art Nouveau at the beginning of the 20th century. Furthermore, industrialization facilitated the arrival of goods and new ideas on a larger scale.

Weapons

Acquired through the Gestoso and Aguiar donations, the Museum's collection of weapons consists of rapiers, daggers, sabres and ceremonial swords made between the 16th and 19th centuries.

From the 16th and 17th centuries are a number of swords for everyday use of the common European type whose main difference is evident in the development of the guards to protect the hand – from the ribbon- to the shell- and basket-hilt types. Dating from the 17th century are various left-hand daggers and a number of spearheads originally fixed to shafts.

With the adoption of French fashions in the 18th century and higher production of firearms, the use of the rapier fell into decline, being worn only on dress occasions, finally to be replaced by the ceremonial sword and the sabre. When swords became ornamental weapons, craftsmen concentrated on the decoration of the hilt, making them of gold, silver or bronze gilt often adorned with ivory, jade and precious stones.

The Museum's collection of firearms has been on loan to the Museo de Artes y Costumbres Populares since 1972.

Furniture

This collection consists of a wide variety of Spanish furniture and includes items such as benches, chairs, chests, tables, console tables and drawing-room furniture. The largest group is of vargeños and secrétaires.

Room VI contains a writing table of the last third of the 17th century whose design is typical of that period. The upper part behind the drop front is made up of three vertical sections, those on the sides being symmetrical and with drawers flanking the central section, which is more richly adorned and consists of a door with smaller drawers behind. Of polychrome and gilded wood, this piece is carved with vegetal motifs and encircled stars and was clearly influenced by the popular Mudéjar crafts.

Another exceptional piece of furniture in the collection is the piano exhibited in Room X. Dated *c.* 1670, it was apparently one of the first Italian-style pieces with Chinese motifs of this type made in Spain.

Embroidery

The 17th century saw the culmination of ecclesiastic embroidery. From the González Abreu donation the Museum possesses a cope and two sets of vestments, each consisting of a chasuble and two dalmatics. Of crimson velvet, two of these four dalmatics are embroidered with religious motifs, the gold of which forms a vertical band running down the middle of the chasuble and along the skirts and cuffs of the dalmatics. Fully Baroque, the third reveals a major change in adornment as the religious motifs are replaced by naturalistic ones embroidered in coloured silks over the whole of the material, which in this case is white satin.

To end this small collection are a sacrament cloth and a 19th-century chasuble of unknown provenance. Both are of white satin embroidered with gold.

Documents

This collection consists of various letters patent of nobility. These were public documents by means of which the King was requested to recognize the petitioner's noble blood and grant the corresponding exemptions and privileges. Handwritten on parchment, they are adorned with miniatures drawn with a quill.

WRITING DESK. (LAST THIRD OF THE 16TH CENTURY).

BIBLIOGRAFÍA

Angulo, D., Juan de la Roelas aportaciones para su estudio. *Archivo Español de Arte y Arqueología, Y, 1925.*

Angulo, D., *Murillo y su escuela.* Seville. 1975.

Angulo, D., *Murillo. Su vida, su arte, su obra.* 3 vols. Madrid, 1981

Arias de Cossio, A. M., *José Gutierrez de la Vega.* Madrid, 1978.

Ayala Mayory, N., *Painting in Seville 1650-1700.* Princeton, 1982.

Banda y Vargas, A., Miscelánea de Pintura Española decimonónica. *Boletín de Bellas Artes,* n. 4, Seville, 1976.

Banda y Vargas, A., *Murillo y la pintura sevillana de su tiempo.* Seville, 1983.

Baticle, J., *Zurbarán: Panorama de su vida y de su obra.* Madrid, 1988.

Bermejo, E., *La Pintura de los primitivos flamencos en España.* Instituto Diego Velázquez, Madrid, 1981.

Beruete y Moret, A., *Valdés Leal, Estudio Crítico.* Madrid, 1911.

Boutelou, C., Noticia de ocho pinturas del s. XV que se conservan en la Iglesia de San Benito de Calatrava en Seville. *Museo Español de Antigüedades,* Vol. IX, 1978.

Brown, J., *Zurbarán.* New York, 1973.

Brown, J., *La Edad de Oro en la pintura española.* London, 1990

Cascales Muño, J., *Las Bellas Artes Plásticas en Sevilla.* Toledo, 1929.

Cena Bermúdez, J.A., *Diccionario Histórico de los más ilustres profesores de las Bellas Artes en España.* Madrid, 1800.

Cherry, P., Arte y Naturaleza. *El Bodegón español en el siglo de Oro.* Madrid, 1999.

Cuellar Contreras, F., Maestros pintores de la escuela sevillana del siglo XVII. Nuevas aportaciones documentales. *Revista de Arte Sevillano*, II, 1982.

Díaz Padrón, M., La obra de Pierre Van Lint en España. *Goya,* 145, pp. 2-9, 1978.

Díaz Padrón, M., Nuevas pinturas de Vicente Sellaer identificadas en el Museo de Bellas Artes de Sevilla y colecciones madrileñas. *Archivo Español de Arte,* 1981.

Díaz Padrón, M., Nuevas pinturas del Maestro del papagayo identificadas en colecciones españolas y extranjeras. *Archivo Español de Arte*, 1984.

Fernández López, J., La Pintura de Historia en Sevilla en el siglo XIX. *Arte Hispalense,* 1985.

Fernández López, J., *Programas iconográficos de la pintura barroca sevillana del siglo XVII.* Seville, 1991.

Fuente, V. de la, Biografía del Dr. D. José Duaso y Latre. Madrid, 1850.

Gestoso Pérez, J., Catálogo de las pinturas y esculturas del Museo Provincial de Sevilla. Seville, 1912.

Gómez Imaz, M., Inventario de los cuadros sustraídos por el gobierno intruso en Sevilla. Año 1810. Seville, 1844.

González de León, F., Noticia histórica y curiosa de los edificios públicos, sagrados y profanos de esta muy noble, muy heróica e invicta ciudad de Sevilla. Seville, 1844, 2ª ed. 1973.

Gudiol, J., Goya. Biografía. Estudio analítico y catálogo de sus pinturas. 4 vols., Barcelona, 1970.

Guerrero Lovillo, J., Los pintores románticos sevillanos. *Archivo Hispalense*, 1949.

Guerrero Lovillo, J., La pintura sevillana en el siglo XVIII. *Archivo Hispalense,* 1955.

Guerrero Lovillo, J., *Antonio María Esquivel.* Madrid, 1957.

Guerrero Lovillo, J., *Valeriano Bécquer.* Seville, 1974.

Guinar, P., *Zurbarán y la pintura española de la vida monástica.* Madrid, 1967.

Heredia Moreno, M. C., Noticias sobre pintores sevillanos de comienzos del siglo XVIII. En *Homenaje al Profesor Hernández Díaz*, 1982, T.I. pp. 423-443.

Hernández Díaz, J., Guía del Museo Provincial de Bellas Artes de Sevilla. Madrid, 1967.

Izquierdo, R., Muñoz, V., Museo de Bellas Artes. Inventario de Pinturas. Seville, 1990.

Kinkead, D. T., *Valdés Leal.* New York, 1978.

Kinkead, D. T., Pintores flamencos en la Sevilla de Murillo. *Archivo Hispalense*, 1981.

López Martínez, C., *Valdés Leal y sus discípulos.* 1907.

López Martínez, C., *La pintura sevillana en el siglo XVIII.* Seville, 1914.

Martínez Ripoll, A., *Francisco de Herrera el Viejo.* Seville, 1978.

Mayer, A., *Murillo.* Berlin, 1913.

Mayer, A., *La pintura española.* Barcelona, 1913.

Merchan Cantisan, R., *El Dean López Cepero y su colección pictórica.* Seville, 1979.

Navarrete Prieto, B., Textos de la Exposición: "Zurbarán y su obrador: pinturas para el Nuevo Mundo". Museo de Bellas Artes de Valencia. 1998.

Navarrete Prieto, B., *La pintura andaluza del siglo XVII y sus fuentes grabadas.* Madrid, 1998.

Ortiz de Zúñiga, D., Anales eclesiásticos y seculares de la muy noble y muy leal ciudad de Sevilla. 5 vols. Madrid, 1795-1796.

Ossorio y Bernard, M., *Galería biográfica de artistas españoles del siglo XIX.* Madrid, 1884.

Pacheco, F., *Arte de la Pintura: su antigüedad y grandeza.* Seville, 1649. Quoted in Sánchez Cantón, Madrid, 1956.

Pantorba, B., *Artistas Andaluces.* Madrid, 1929.

Pantorba, B., *Historia y crítica de las Exposiciones Nacionales de Bellas Artes celebradas en España.* Madrid, 1948.

Pardo Canalis, E., Bosquejo histórico de D. José Duaso. In *Anales del Instituto de Estudios Madrileños,* 1966.

Pemán, C., Un retablo sevillano en la colección Orleáns de Sanlúcar. *Archivo Español de Arte y Arqueología.* VI, 1930.

Pérez Calero. G., *El pintor Eduardo Cano de la Peña. (1823-1897).* Seville, 1979.

Pérez Calero. G., José Jiménez Aranda. *Arte Hispalense.* 1982.

Pérez Sánchez, A., *Pintura italiana del siglo XVII en España.* Madrid, 1965.

Pérez Sánchez, A., Sobre bodegones italianos, napolitanos especialmente. *Archivo Español de Arte,* 1967, pp. 316 and following pages.

Pleguezuelo Hernández, A., *Azulejo sevillano.* Seville, 1989.

Ponz, A., Viaje de España, en que se da noticia de las cosas mas apreciables y dignas de saberse, que hay en ella. Madrid, 1772-1794. Re-edited 1972.

Post, CH. R., *A History of Spanish Painting.* 15 vols. Cambridge, Massachusets, 1930-1958.

Reina Palazón, A., *La pintura costumbrista en Sevilla. (1830-1870).* Seville, 1979.

Sambricio, V., *Velázquez y lo velazqueño.* Madrid, 1960.

Sánchez Cantón, F. J., *La vida de San Pedro Nolasco. Pinturas del Claustro del Refectorio de la Merced Calzada de Sevilla.* Seville, 1922.

Sánchez Cantón, F. J., Goya, refugiado. *Goya,* 3, pp. 130-134, 1954.

Sánchez Pineda, C., Los cuadros de la Máscara de la Real Fábrica de Tabacos de Sevilla. *Boletín de la Real Academia de Buenas Letras de Sevilla,* 1944.

Serrera, J. M., Un nuevo cuadro de Francisco de Herrera el Mozo. *Revista de Arte Sevillano,* III, 1983.

Serrera, J. M., Vasco Pereira, un pintor portugués en la Sevilla del siglo XVI. *Archivo Hispalense* LXX, 213, 1987.

Serrera, J. M., / Valdivieso, E., *Pintura sevillana del primer tercio del siglo XVII.* Madrid, 1985.

Valdivieso, E., *Pintura sevillana del siglo XIX.* Seville, 1981.

Valdivieso, E., *Historia de la pintura sevillana siglos XII al XX.* Seville, 1986.

Valdivieso, E., Dos nuevas pinturas de Francisco Gutierres. *Revista de Arte Sevillano,* II, 1982.

Valdivieso, E., Francisco Gutiérrez, pintor de perspectiva. *Boletín del Museo del Prado,* 9, pp. 175-180, 1982.

Valdivieso, E., *Juan de Valdés Leal.* Seville, 1988.

Various authors, Museo de Bellas Artes de Sevilla. T. I, II. Seville, 1991.

COORDINATION AND PRODUCTION
Aldeasa

COVER ILLUSTRATION
Bartolomé E. Murillo, *SS. Justa and Rufina* (detail)

TRANSLATION
Nigel Williams

DESIGN
Aldeasa

LAYOUT
Myriam López Consalvi

PHOTOGRAPHS
Museo de Bellas Artes Archives

Aldeasa Archives

Pedro Feria / Alberto Sánchez

PHOTOMECHANICAL PRODUCTION
Lucam

PRINTED BY
Jomagar

First edition September 2000
ISBN Consejería de Cultura: 84-8266-178-7
ISBN Aldeasa: 84-8003-978-7
LEGAL DEPOSIT: M-25719-2002